Sharps Rifle

The Gun That Shaped American Destiny

By Martin Rywell

Library of Congress Catalog Card Number 56-12177

CONTENTS

APPENDIX

CHAPTER I

Guns in American History
By Martin Rywell

The American experiment was made possible by the gun and was made successful by the lesson taught by the gun manufacture-mass production with the machine. The gun found the earliest manifestation of orderly planning and of the manipulation of a number of identical units. This essential change in manufacture is the difference between industry and handicraft. It is due far less to the different nature of the tools employed in each than to the subdivision in one and the undivided control by a single workman in the other. This factor dominates American production and is the cornerstone of our economy.

It was introduced by Eli Whitney when in 1798 he received a government contract for muskets. He designed and developed machine-tools to turn out uniform parts that were interchangeable. Guns were up to this time the product of a gunsmith. The gunmaker was a master craftsman who served an apprentice-ship and who knew how to do most of the work. However an arm was seldom the work of one man. It was the work of the barrel maker, lock maker, spring maker, stocker, mounter, engraver and other specialists. The gunmaker knew how to finish and repair the weapon. None of the parts were interchangeable or produced by machinery. Whitney's innovation was that he would replace individually made muskets with thousands of mass-produced, standardized muskets with interchangeable parts. After years of designing machinery Whitney produced each musket to consist of fifty distinct parts and each interchangeable with other muskets. We therefore concluded that the gun fathered the concept which was to become the American Industrial system as it was translated into other fields.

America was a new nation born in the throes of a social revolution that was made possible by the gun. Feudalism was passing and Capitalism was being developed by the man of the middle station. He had to challenge the power of the church-state, free himself of a society of the past and commit himself to a future of provable truth. Man questioned old values and the gun was the questioner's right. The gun had only been invented during the latter half of the 14th century and was slowly being developed and introduced.

The American pioneer came to a cold and hostile wilderness. His first task was self-sustenance, clothing, and self-defense. The earliest American architecture was the fortress or block enclosure. The colonist brought his primitive European weapon to kill game for food and clothing and to protect himself from the Indian. The European weapon failed to meet the demands of the American environment because the weapon was too heavy and its bore too large. The European fowling piece of the 1700's was little more than the refined large barreled musket. In Central Europe the game was deer rather than the feather and the sporting weapon was shorter than the French, English and Spanish models. The early shotguns were usually long barreled pieces with full length wooden stocks. About 1725 there developed about Lancaster, Pennsylvania a weapon known as the Kentucky rifle. It acquired its name because it was used extensively in Kentucky but it was a development of the European firearm adapted to meet the demands of the American environment.

Discovery of a new continent and with rival imperialism of the old world trying to grasp it and hold it in the teeth of nature and the natives required the tenacity of the gun. The rivalry found expression on the new continent in King William's War, Queen Anne's War, King George's War, the French and Indian War, and Pontiac's Conspiracy.

European artisans of great competence were among the new immigrants to America. By 1763 two-thirds of the Americans were new men and not the sons or grandsons of earlier settlers. This new blood that came into colonial streams was from West Germany, North Ireland, French Huguenots, and other peoples. The gunsmiths about Lancaster, Pennsylvania were chiefly Swiss and German and they developed the design of the Kentucky rifle for American needs.

Major Pollard of England writes, "The outbreak of the American war of Independence brought us into contact with a new military phenomenon—the rifled armed sharpshooter far beyond the compass of the army musket. The Americans had evolved a new type of arm suited to their environment. They needed a reliable, accurate hunting weapon efficient for use against Indians, and of small caliber. They had to go into the forests on long trips, carrying with them their supply of powder and ball. Weight was virtually important and had to be reduced as far as possible. Accuracy was essential, as life might hang on a shot. To meet the demands of the colonists, their own gunsmiths evolved a special weapon known generically as the Kentucky rifle. The typical weapon had a forty-two inch barrel, weighed about nine pounds, and carried a half-ounce ball of thirty-two to the pound. They had long octagonal barrels and slender stocks of maple wood fitted with a curved or recessed heel plate and a patch box."

The secret of the Kentucky rifle's value lay not so much in their accuracy, which was good rather than remarkable, but in the simple trick of loading. The European riflemen used a tightly fitting lead ball which he slammed down hard with ramrod or mallet and rod until it expanded to fit the grooves of the weapon. The American simply wrapped his bullet, which was small, in a greased leather circular patch. Reloading a fouled rifle was no trouble to him. His loosely fitting projectile could be pushed home as swiftly as a ball could be wadded into a smooth bore. The patch lubricated the bore and took up all space which otherwise would be free to let explosion gases pass the ball.

England imported regiments of German Hessians during the American Revolution. The Hessians carried big bore cumbrous hunting weapons, extremely heavy and filled with hair trigger, complex sights, some even with telescopic sights, clumsy butt with check piece, patch box and crotch heel plate.

Stages of American progress in the conquest of a continent are interestingly shown in firearms. American experience developed its own patterns. The Kentucky rifle with flintlock ignition, the Plains rifle with percussion, the breech-loading Sharps, the Colt revolver, the repeating Winchester, the Derringer, the pepperbox, the Smith & Wesson, the Remington, all modified by the frontier as the pioneer jostled for elbow room and moved across a continent.

Exploration had moved settlements out of the Eastern forested areas into the plains and the mountains. Beyond the costal plain closed by the Appalachians lay a region larger than all of France, Germany and Poland. Empty land stretched westward, forests stood virgin thick and no barrier of status stopped a man.

By 1840 there developed the short, heavy, large caliber Plains rifle because the Kentucky rifle of small bore was not adequate against the buffalo and its long barrel awkward to handle from the saddle astride a horse.

In the meantime a Scotch clergyman, Alexander Forsyth had invented the percussion lock to replace the flintlock. Conical bullets were being developed to replace the round ball. A breech-loader was being sought to replace the muzzle-loader.

Christian Sharps appeared with the answer in his single-shot breech-loading gun invented in 1848.

Rifled arms had been made sporadically since 1540 but lacked general appreciation. The smooth bore persisted for military service because the thick fouling with black powder obstructed the rifling so that a tight fitting ball could not be easily rammed down. If the ball did not fit tightly it did not take the advantage of the grooves and was in effect a smooth bore. The solution was apparent in the breech-loader.

The introduction of a charge at the breech was old. Loose powder was dangerous with wheel-lock or flint ignition. Percussion changed this with priming no longer necessary. The success of the breech-loader was not dependent on any mechanical perfection but entirely on the invention of the metallic cartridge case. The metal would expand under the gaseous pressure when the gun was discharged and would fit tightly in the rifling grooves.

An intermediate step in the development of the metallic cartridge was the wide use of breech loaders using paper cartridges fired by an independent cap or tape primer. Later these arms were remodelled or converted to take true metallic cartridges. The Sharps rifle is the most important of these actions because it was one of the soundest mechanically and made a very fine cartridge rifle. In this intermediate step from paper to metal, oddities followed as patentees sought the answer in peculiar cartridges and separate caps but the answer was in the expandable metallic cartridge case.

CHAPTER II

The Sharps Gun in American History

Two influences have been of prime importance in the rise of the United States from a mere handful of settlers to the leading world power. These are the forces of the frontier and sectionalism and in both Sharps guns played an important part, as well as represented a major development in firearms.

Western Emigration

Sharps guns accompanied every wagon train from the Mississippi to the Rio Grande, the Sacramento, or the Columbia during the 1850s and 1860s and it is said to have taught alike Pawnee, Ute, Arapahoe, Cheyenne, Sioux, Crow and Blackfoot that their canutelike attempts to check the incoming tide of white men were predestined to be a losing game. An Indian, American Horse, comments: "Emigrants passing up the South Platte River to Colorado between 1858 and 1865 were largely armed with Sharps military rifles."

Kansas

In the struggle for Kansas, whether it be admitted as a slave state or free state and a rehearsal of the Civil War, Sharps rifles won nationwide fame as "Beecher's Bibles" after Reverend Henry Ward Beecher said, he saw more "Moral power in one of these instruments as far as the slaveholders were concerned than in a hundred Bibles."

Kansas is the story of ruffians, rebellion and rifle. The rifle is the Sharps. It introduced violence as the solution of sectionalism and thus became the opening battle of the Civil War.

6

The Kansas-Nebraska Law of 1854 declared that the settlers had the right to determine whether their state be slave or free. The North and South tried to secure control of Kansas.

Massachusetts, one of the important protagonists in sectionalism spearheaded a mass moral movement of emigration to Kansas. The Massachusetts Emigrant Aid Society, later superseded by the New England Emigrant Aid Society, sent settlers to Kansas in an unique social experiment because it was an organized immigration cloaked with morality.

Eli Thayer, prime organizer of this movement, writes: "I know that many Sharps rifles went along with the emigrants sent by the company, and these men knew how to use them when the emergency demanded, as those familiar with Kansas history well know. No organization openly provided such implements at first, but they generally formed a part of the equipment of our colonists. The directors furnished them on individual responsibility. Mr. Amos Lawrence and others of the Company provided a large quantity of arms and ammunition and sent them to Kansas in 1855. Dr. Robinson's firm and decided policy, and the fact that the settlers were well armed with Sharps rifles and ready to use them caused the retreat of the Missourians from Lawrence in December 1855."

In 1855, Amos Lawrence, President of the New England Emigrant Aid Society, also an uncle of President Franklin Pierce, entered in his journal: "Paid $1,000 —for rifles for Kansas sufferers" and to the Secretary in July he wrote, "get terms for one hundred more of the Sharps rifles at once."

Dr. Robinson, secretary of the Company, wrote to Lawrence in December 1855, "Thank you and the friends who sent us the Sharps rifles . . . we need, however, one or two hundred more of the same sort." Beginning in 1855, Sharps rifles and carbines were supplied to the anti-slavery men in Kansas.

John Brown

John Brown used Sharps carbines in his raid on Harpers Ferry Arsenal in 1859 in his plan to arouse a slave insurrection.

John Brown took unto himself God's will as sanction for his acts to abolish slavery. The end justified the means. Blinded to the possible consequence of his acts, he failed to understand that the means can produce consequences worse than the end evil. Among his acts was that on the night of May 24, 1856, John Brown commanded a party at Pottawatomie Creek, Kansas which took five men from their homes and killed them. Brown had become an outstanding free-state partisan hero of Kansas warfare.

When peace was restored in Kansas 200 Sharps carbines that had been sold by the Sharps Rifle Manufacturing Co. to the Massachusetts Committee were stopped in transit and stored in Tabor, Iowa, an abolitionist stronghold. The Massachusetts committee turned these carbines over to Brown for "safe-keeping".

Using these carbines on Sunday night, October 16, 1859, John Brown led a raid on Harpers Ferry Arsenal to seize the weapons and start a slave insurrection. Colonel Robert E. Lee, of later fame captured Brown. 102 of these Sharps carbines were recovered and stored in Harpers Ferry Arsenal. Shortly after the outbreak of the Civil War, Confederates captured the arsenal and used the Sharps to arm Confederate calvary.

Civil War

Close to 100,000 Sharps rifles and carbines served the Union troops during the Civil War and earned Berdan Sharpshooters their distinction.

In this conflict we may trace the influence of Eli Whitney again. It was the cotton gin invention which had made cotton the leading staple of the South, dependent upon slave labor and the soil.

Colonel Hiram Berdan, a mechanical engineer and for 15 years prior to 1861, the nation's best rifle marksman, appealed through the newspapers for "the best marksmen in the country, to form a corps of skirmishers" under his command. His organization was to be composed of companies of the best marksmen possible of the Northern states and to arm them with the most reliable rifle made.

The government accepted the proposal on June 15, 1861 and the adjutant-generals of the different states issued a call, but that "no man be accepted who cannot, at 200 yards, put ten consecutive shots in a target, the average distance not to exceed five inches from the center of the bullseye." Each man was allowed to choose his own rifle, but must justify his selection by the performance of the weapon in his hands. Many, however, preferred to let the government furnish them.

Aware of the publicity value if their weapons would be adopted, manufacturers of all sorts of weapons offered their guns for trial and acceptance. Colonel Berdan and his men selected the 1859 Sharps, Single-shot, breech-loading rifle, known as the Sharps improved rifle, military pattern.

The Chief of Army Ordnance, James Wolfe Ripley, was very anxious to have the regiment armed with the muzzle-loading Springfield, then the established arm of the U.S. Infantry. But Col. Berdan made a requisition for the breech-loading Sharps which proved to be, according to Berdan, "a declaration of war."

The newspapers contained almost daily statements of what Chief Ripley had to say, or General Scott, or the Assistant Secretary of War Thomas Scott. They took the ground that there was no rifle equal to the Springfield for a soldier, except Chief Ripley, who went so far as to say that he preferred the old smooth bore with "ball and buck". General Scott, in his endorsement of the Berdan's application said, "Breech-loaders would spoil his command."

Col. Berdan persisted in his efforts to obtain the Sharps rifle. The Sharp-shooters wanted the Sharps and so did President Lincoln but Chief Ripley, appointed April 1861, refused to order the Sharps. He did not approve of breech-loaders. Prior to 1861 there were Hall, Colt and Sharps breech-loaders and a very limited quantity of these. Varieties of breech-loaders evolved as the war progressed.

Company A of the Sharpshooters appealed to their Congressmen for help and even promised to pay for the Sharps. But to no avail. In December 1861 a New York Post correspondent visited the Sharpshooters at camp outside Washington and he saw 2,000 men dressed in dark-green uniforms, gray overcoats trimmed with green, and fur-covered knapsacks. Some had brought their own target rifles and only fifty muskets had been issued to them for guard duty. The Correspondent commented: "It is a wonder that the men retain their spirits under such long delay, and it speaks well for their officers that they are not discouraged. Sharps rifles were promised them by the President and ordered by General McClellan, but some trouble in the War Department has thus far prevented their getting them. Let us hope they will soon have the weapon they are so competent to wield."

Simon Cameron's last act as Secretary of War was to sign an order for a contract for 2,000 Sharps rifles for the Berdan Regiment. That was January 13, 1862. Ordnance Chief Ripley stalled, did not order the Sharps but instead ordered 1,000 Colt's revolving rifles. The men of the 2nd Sharpshooter Regiment refused the Colts and threatened to mutiny. The new Secretary of War Stanton finally ordered the Sharps and they took the field in 1862.

The historian of the U.S. Sharpshooters records:

"On May 8th, 1862 the regiment received the long expected Sharps rifles, now needed more than ever, as the Colts were for our dangerous service found defective in many respects, and they gladly turned in the 'five shooters'." On receiving the new arms the men were impatient to get again within shooting distance of the enemy. These rifles shot both linen and skin cartridges, of 52 caliber, and also had primers, little round, flat coppered things, which were inserted below the hammer; but the regular army or hat cap was more generally used, as the primers were not always a 'sure thing'; also carried the angular bayonet."

In the Seven Days Battles of June, July 1862, the Sharpshooters demonstrated the rapid fire of the breech-loader and the advantage of loading while prone. Col. Charles P. Kingsbury, Chief ordnance officer to Gen. McClellan wrote to Chief Ripley: "Berdan's Sharpshooters have demonstrated the value of the breech-loading arms in the hands of skillful troops." Col. Kingsbury was relieved for reasons of "health", demoted to Major, and exiled to the Indian Country.

Historians and generals declared that the attack by Col. Berdan on Longstreet was the turning point of the war. It was July 2, 1863, the second day of the Battle of Gettysburg when Longstreet's men pushed toward Little Round Top when they met one hundred Berdan Sharpshooters supported by two hundred Maine muzzle-loader troops. A 25 minute action followed with each Sharpshooter averaging 95 rounds and thus creating the impression that there were "two Federal regiments". 300 men stopped the forward movement of 30,000 foes. It was an important stand because it delayed Longstreet's men 40 minutes and thereby prevented Longstreet from taking Peach Orchard and the ridge.

Gen. Longstreet said, "If we had got around to Round Top we would have held the key to the situation and could have cut the Union force in two parts, which could not help each other, and then by the force of a sweeping charge we could have won the day."

Gen. Sickles in his Gettysburg address said of the contest at Pitzer's Run, "Where Longstreet was massing his tens of thousands, and where Col. Berdan pushing through the curtain of woods, hurled his dauntless little band directly against the force intended to crush in our left flank and seize the Round Tops"; which statement was endorsed by Gen. Hunt, present, on his personal knowledge of the circumstances.

Gen. Sickles in a subsequent speech said: "In 1886 I met many Confederate officers at Gettysburg, and in conversation with Gen. Longstreet, asked him what his intentions were on that day."

"To take possession of Peach Orchard and the ridge," was the reply.

"What prevented your taking that position at once?"

"Your Sharpshooters, who smoked us out of the woods on your flank."

"When I asked him what would have been the result of the ridge and peach orchard without resistance, he said the Confederates would have won the battle of Gettysburg. He also said that when he reached the ridge and peach orchard his loss was so great by my defense of that position that even with his reinforcements he was not strong enough to win."

In after years on the memorial occasion, Gen. Sickles, in a letter to the survivors, said: "It is not too much to declare that you were able to develop and disclose enough of the position, force, formation and movements of the enemy, to warrant the belief that the battle would be fought on the left, and to justify the dispositions made by me to meet the enemy there. This reconnaissance is historical. It deserves commemoration. It was not only a brilliant feat of arms, it was of inestimable advantage and value to our cause, contributing, as it did, to the decisive victory of July 2nd, from which the enemy never recovered."

A Sharpshooter was captured and taken through the Confederate lines and he adds: "It is impossible for me to describe the slaughter we had made in their ranks. In all my past service, it beat all I have ever seen for the number engaged and for so short a time. They were piled in heaps and across each other. The doctor would hardly believe that there were so few of us fighting them, though we had a corps, as he said, he never saw lead so thick in his life as it was in those woods."

On Sept. 2, 1863 the New York Times reported the forced retirement of Chief of Ordnance Ripley after more than forty-five years service and added, "the old fogy Ripley . . . who combatted all new ideas in the fabrication of firearms, artillery and projectiles."

Between January 1, 1861 and June 30, 1866 the U.S. government bought from the Sharps Rifle Manufacturing Company, 80,512 carbines and 9,141 rifles. Combined the amount of government purchases with some Sharps previously owned, we may conclude that close to 100,000 Sharps were used during the Civil War. 16,306,508 rounds of ammunition for Sharps rifles and carbines were used during the war. Only one breech-loader was ordered in greater quantity than the Sharps and that was the Spencer but mainly in the last year of the war.

A volunteer calvaryman reports, "The Spencer carbine was latterly in very general us, superseding Sharps. There was little to choose between them I have fired as many rounds in the course of twenty minutes out of Sharps as out of Spencer, the latter fired seven rounds pretty rapidly, but it takes some time to reload."

The Sharps rifle, model 1859, had a vertical slidong breech-block that was worked by a lever under the gun. To load the gun, the lever was pulled down, a 54 caliber paper cartridge was inserted and the lever pushed up. Sharps rifle could be fired three times as fast as a rifle that was loaded at the muzzle. Groove diameters varied during the war. A special type of bullet was designed to be used in all of them. The body diameter was only .53 inch but the rear $\frac{1}{8}$ of its length was .56 inch in diameter. In 1860 the standard powder charge was 50 grains of black powder. The regulation sheet for an old style paper wrapper was a paper trapezoid with a 3 inch base and two sides, one side was 2.25 inches and the other side was 3.25 inches. The metallic cartridge Sharps was introduced after the end of the war.

Capt. Charles Augustus Stevens, Historian of Berdan's U.S. Sharpshooters writes: "The open-sighted Sharps rifle, using linen or 'skin' cartridges, 52 caliber, conical ball, was the best breech-loading gun at that time made, a perfectly safe and reliable arm, combining accuracy with rapidity, just what a skirmish line needed for effective work. To their good judgment in choosing this rifle may be attributed their future success in the field, attaining as they did a reputation that eventually made the name of 'Berdan Sharpshooters' renowned in foreign lands as well as our own. The muzzle-loading target rifles—telescopic and globe sights—while of great value before fortifications and for special work, would have been useless in skirmishing."

Silas W. Howard, a Sharpshooter, was wounded and he did not expect to survive. He took out the fire-block of his Sharps and threw it away so that no Confederate could use the rifle. Perhaps others did likewise.

The Confederates could not use the Sharps arms that they captured because it required special ammunition and they did not have the special ammunition. A Confederate copy of Sharps was made by S. C. Robinson Arms Manufacturing Co. of Richmond, Virginia but it was a defective imitation. It was made with a block movement perpendicular to the barrel axis. The lock plate and barrel were marked, "S. C. Robinson Arms Mfg. Co., Richmond, Va., 1862" and followed with a serial number.

There were some unmarked Confederate Sharps which did not have the bar and swivel ring on the left side of the gun.

A Confederate Lieutenant of Cavalry in 1863 reported, "Forty new Sharps rifles with Richmond stamp on them were handed yesterday to my company. The men were ordered to test them. Nine were fired, and seven of the nine burst."

Popular Revolver

Sharps was the leader in the cartridge pepperbox. Sharps produced the 4-barreled cartridge to meet the demand for a popular-priced revolver and to compete with Smith and Wesson who had a monopoly by virtue of the basic Rollin White patent. Sharps produced more cartridge pepperbox revolvers than the combined output of all other American makers.

Buffalo Carbine

The Sharps enjoyed the preference among professional buffalo hunters particularly after the long range metallic cartridge models were introduced in 1871. Killing off the bison was a military method to hold the Plains Indians on their reservations where they had a meat supply. Sharps carbine was the favorite of the buffalo hunter after the war as the vast herds that roamed the Western plains were exterminated.

The buffalo, the American Bison, once roamed the open prairies most of which is now our nation in vast herds that were estimated to be in the millions. The region of the buffalo's best adaptation was the Great Plains that lie beween the Rocky Mountains and the bend of the Missouri out of Dakota and reach from Canada as far as the Pecos in Texas.

The Great Plains is half the size of all the United States lying east of the Mississippi and is cut by a succession of east-flowing streams. The buffaloes climbed northward in the spring and descended in the fall, moving from river to river. The whole economy of the Plains Indian tribes was based upon the buffalo because all the parts of the animal were used; it was almost their sole subsistence—shelter, clothing, food and fuel.

In 1492 the present United States held perhaps little over 250,000 Indians while the buffalo was estimated from fifty to one hundred and twenty-five million. In 1880, the buffalo was estimated at forty million.

In 1850, the buffalo had dwindled to about twenty million. The thunder of the buffaloes' running hoofs shook the earth. In 1859 Horace Greeley, New York Tribune editor, went West and reported, "We are in sight of millions of buffaloes. What strikes the stranger with most amazement is their immense numbers. I know a million is a great many, but I am confident, we saw that number. Often, the country for miles on either hand seemed quite black with them."

Between 1870 and 1875 it is estimated twelve and a half million buffalo were killed in Nebraska, Kansas, Indian Territory and Texas. Killing buffalo had become a major international sport. Buffalo robes became a stylish rage. Tom Nixon, a prominent professional buffalo hunter, burned out the barrel of a Sharps killing one hundred and twenty buffaloes in forty minutes.

The Sharps Big Fifty was the favorite weapon. The next best were the Sharps 45-70, 45-90, and 45-120. The technique of the skillful hunter was to drop one "lead" buffalo after another with clean neck or heart shots. A wounded animal was sure to stampede the herd into wild flight. Hence the value of the **Big Fifty** Sharps was because it usually killed with one bullet if the bullet was properly placed. A full-grown buffalo bull stood six feet high at the shoulder with a length of nine and one half feet and weighed about 2500 pounds.

In 1889 only 541 buffalo remained.

In 1893 the wild ones were hunted down until only 20 buffalo remained.

The Indians had been starved into subjection.

Buffalo Jones, who used a Sharps to kill bison, wrote: "The buffalo hunters conquered the whole Indian race—not by unerring aim at the red devils themselves —while perchance they encircled the camp, or in combat when they often met; but simply by slaying the buffalo and thereby cutting off their source of supplies."

John P. Lower in the 1876 edition of the Denver City Directory has the following advertisement: Sharps Creedmoor Rifles . . . $75 to $125. Sporting 40, 44, 45, & 50 caliber . . . $35 to $75; Hunters 40, 44, 45, & 50 cal. $30 to $40; Needle 40, 44, 45, & 50 cal . . . $28 to $30; and Needle carbines 50 cal . . . $25 and continued "Among the principal improved Fire Arms kept constantly on hand are the Sharps Rifles of various styles, which have proved to be the best in the world for long range shooting."

The western railroads brought professional buffalo hunters because the military suggested that killing off the bison would hold the Plains Indians on their reservations where the only meat supply remained.

Texas Ranger
The vigilantes and the Rangers used the Sharps to enforce frontier justice, and when the Texas Rangers were reactivated in 1874, the Sharps carbine, 50 caliber, known as the "Lead Belly" was the first official gun of the rangers.

Railroad Building
Building of the railroads through Indian Country needed the protection of U.S. Cavalry whose official arm until 1873 was the Sharps carbine. Therefore the Sharps can claim the Winning of the West because it helped the push westward by the railroads and by the recession of the Indians.

Cattle
The 50 caliber Sharps was the cattleman's weapon. In 1865 Confederate soldiers returned to Texas to find cattle running wild in unfenced areas and having indeed multiplied. After the war many people had moved westward, set up new ranches and needed cattle. The East needed meat. Texas cattle brought two or three dollars per head but up in Dodge or some other markets they sold for twenty or thirty dollars per head. The Western, the Chisolm, the Loving and many other routes were used to drive the herds to market. The herd could be lost by Indian attack as well as by storm or stampede. Texas needed trail drivers and their primary qualification was to know how to shoot straight. The Sharps carbine had emerged from the Civil War as a fine saddle gun for frontier use and it was the cattleman's tool not only to aid the trail driver but also to protect the ranches from rustling or encroachment.

Custer's Last Stand
In the heated afternoon of June 25, 1876 Col. George Armstrong Custer rode into the valley of the Little Big Horn in Montana with five companies of the

7th Cavalry. All were annihilated by Sioux Indians and history records it as Custer's Last Stand. The report of the Secretary of War states that the five companies had 405 Springfield carbines cal. 45 along with single action 396 Colt revolvers cal. 45 but did not have any Sharps carbines. Much criticism of the Springfield was later expressed.

G. B. Grinnell in The Fighting Cheyennes writes, "When the fight began about half the Indians had guns and the remainders bows . . . the guns were of many sorts—muzzle loaders, Spencer carbines, old-fashioned Henry rifles, and old Sharps military rifles. The Sharps were probably the best guns they had, except those recently captured from the soldiers." Indians acquired Sharps by trade or capture. When Little Wolf leading a band of thirty-three North Cheyenne warriors surrendered on March 25, 1879, they gave up twenty assorted rifles and carbines of which the majority of any make were Sharps that numbered nine.

CHAPTER III

Christian Sharps & Sharps Rifle Manufacturing Company

Christian Sharps was born in Washington, New Jersey in 1811. The facts about his life are tantalizingly slim. At the age of 19, he began to work for Captain John Harris Hall at Harpers Ferry Arsenal.

The United States government set up two national armories—one at Springfield and another at Harpers Ferry. Harpers Ferry Arsenal, at the confluence of the Potomac and Shenandoah rivers in the easternmost West Virginia was established in 1796 and derives its name from Robert Harper who in 1747 had set up a ferry service across the river.

Captain Hall of Portland, Maine on May 21, 1811, had been granted a patent for a breech-loading rifle. Adopted by the United States, it was the first breech-loader officially adopted by any army. In 1819 Hall received a government contract to manufacture his rifle at Harpers Ferry Armory. Capt. Hall following in the Whitney system of interchangeable parts had written to the government that, "I shall attempt to make every similar part of every gun so much alike that it will suit every gun, so that if a thousand guns were taken apart and the limbs thrown promiscuously together in one heap, they may be taken promiscuously from the heap and will all come right." Startling because of the manufacturing innovation and remarkable because he uses "a thousand" as an example when the Springfield Armory in two years after its organization in 1792 had produced only 245 muskets. Hall designed the machinery to produce his gun and all the equipment at Harpers Ferry was at his disposal.

The Hall rifle consisted of a plain central hammer box lock enclosed in a case behind a chamber. The whole action, lock, chamber and all, was pivoted in a box frame at the rear of the barrel. Pressure on a short lever under the fore-end lifted the chamber, which had radically grooved locking blocks on its side, so that its mouth was tilted above the barrel to receive the charge. It used flintlock ignition.

Major H. B. C. Pollard writes: "It is not improbable that the Hall rifle was one of the great factors influencing Samuel Colt. The early Colt revolving rifles of 1836 have a hammerless action operated by a lever similar to that used to elevate the Hall chamber, and there are one or two other small suggestions which indicate the influence of Hall's ideas."

Christian Sharps employed at Harpers Ferry under Captain Hall was subjected to both the influence of the system of interchangeable parts and the breech-loader. In 1853 Colt, a disciple of Whitney, built his armory at Hartford, employed 369 persons and utilizing the interchangeable parts method. The Sharps Armory was erected in 1860 in Hartford, with 300 persons and also adherents to the new system.

About 1844 the Harpers Ferry Arsenal closed and Sharps moved to Cincinnati, Ohio. He is not listed in the Cincinnati Directory of the period but he lists Cincinnati in his patent application of 1848.

Christian Sharps was issued patent No. 5763 on September 12, 1848 for a single-shot breech-loading gun. A movable breech block slid downward when the trigger guard was moved forward. It exposed the breech end of the barrel. Then a linen cartridge was inserted in the receiver. When the sharp edge of the breech block was brought back in the firing position, it sheared off the rear end of the cartridge and exposed the powder. A percussion cap fired the arm. It was possible to load and fire about five times a minute.

About 1850 Christian Sharps moved to Mill Creek, Pennsylvania, near Philadelphia and contracted the Sharps rifle manufacture to the Nippes Works. The Nippes family were arms makers. They had received a contract in 1808 for manufacture of the 1808 model U.S. musket when the contract was awarded to Winner, Nippes and Steinman. In 1842 the Nippes family received a contract for the Model 1840 muskets.

Sharps rifles were also contracted by Robbins and Lawrence of Windsor, Vermont, Maynard Gun Co. and Mass. Arms Co. of Chicopee Falls, Massachusetts.

Sharps submitted his gun to the Army Ordnance Board and after testing it, they reported on November 27, 1850: "From the observations of the use of this rifle, the Board is of the opinion that it is superior to any of the other arms loading at the breech, and think it would be well to have further trials made, and to put some of them in the hands of troops to determine whether they are suitable to the military service."

In 1851 Sharps Rifle Manufacturing Company was organized at Hartford, Connecticut with a capital of one hundred thousand dollars. John C. Palmer was elected President and Treasurer, Daniel Penfield, Secretary, M. W. Chapin, James Goodwin, S. E. Robbins, and William T. Lee as directors. Christian Sharps was to serve as technical advisor and to receive a royalty of one dollar for each gun manufactured.

Three months after the Sharps Rifle Manufacturing Company was organized Robbins and Lawrence of Windsor, Vermont organized a separate partnership in Hartford to manufacture all rifles for Sharps Rifle Manufacturing Company. Robbins and Lawrence acquired a twenty-five acre tract and built a factory. Richard S. Lawrence moved to Hartford to supervise the work. Robbins & Lawrence were then outstanding in the design of machine tools and interchangeable parts manufacture.

Richard Smith Lawrence perhaps was responsible for the formation of the Sharps Manufacturing Company but he definitely was responsible for the development of the Sharps Rifle.

He contributed five patents. Patent No. 8637 granted 1852 relating to breech-loading, 22958 granted 1859 rear-sight, 23590 granted 1859 pellet cut-off for Sharps primer, 26504 granted 1859 flanged plate gas check, 88645 granted 1869 relating to firearm.

Christian Sharps served as advisor to the Sharps Rifle Manufacturing Company until 1853 when he severed his connection, moved to Philadelphia, and went into business as C. Sharps & Co.

Richard S. Lawrence was born in Vermont in 1817. He learned gunmaking in the shop of his uncle, Asa Story, in Windsor, Vermont. He then worked for Nicanor Kendall, a gun manufacturer, who had a contract to use the prison labor at Windsor prison along with free mechanics. Kendall then manufactured a five shot under-hammer percussion rifle with a sliding breech block. In 1843 Kendall gave up rifle manufacturing and formed a partnership with Lawrence to do custom gun work. In 1844 Samuel E. Robbins, a retired promoter, obtained a government contract for ten thousand Model 1841 Army rifles. Robbins became a partner and the firm name was changed to Robbins, Kendall and Lawrence. After the completion of the contract Robbins and Lawrence bought out Kendall's interest. They obtained a contract for 15,000 more rifles, and in 1851 sent six of these rifles to the Crystal Palace Exhibition in London. These rifles manufactured with interchangeable parts were a revelation to England and resulted in a contract to Robbins and Lawrence for machinery for the new English Arsenal.

In 1854 a report of tests under Col. Huger at Harpers Ferry noted: "The bullets are too large for the diameter of chamber of barrel. After being fired four or five rounds, it was found impossible to force the cartridge in without bursting it and spilling the powder. The firing was continued by resorting to the expedient of separating the bullet from the cartridge, forcing it into the chamber with a stick, and afterwards pouring in the powder. The slide frequently became very difficult to move. When the arm was taken into the shop to be cleaned after the firing concluded, the slide could not be moved at all until thoroughly soaked in oil to soften the dirt around it. The paper cartridge is always left behind in the chamber after each shot, and is frequently in fire when the succeeding cartridge is inserted. To remove all likelihood of danger from this, the paper remaining in the chamber after each shot was removed before inserting another cartridge."

Lawrence moved to Hartford in 1852 to supervise the manufacture of the Sharps rifles. In 1856 Robbins and Lawrence failed due to legal entanglements of a contract with Britain for gun manufacture and the unexpected ending of the Crimean War in 1856. Lawrence then assumed the position of Master Armorer for the Sharps Rifle Manufacturing Company.

In 1853 Sharps left the Sharps Rifle Manufacturing Company of Hartford, Connecticut and returned to Philadelphia.

There is no evidence that Christian Sharps was ever again connected with the Sharps Rifle Manufacturing Co. though his brother-in-law, Robert Chadwick, is reported to have taken charge of the Sharps Cartridge factory in 1851.

The U.S. Army ordered 200 carbines on July 28, 1854 and these were issued to the 1st U.S. Dragoons in 1854 and 1855. In 1855 Great Britain ordered carbines and these were issued to the British cavalry. The British government contract was for carbines patterned after 1852 model Sharps but with the Maynard primer.

During 1855 and 1856 about 1000 Sharps rifles and carbines were supplied to the anti-slavery men in Kansas territory by the New England Emigrant Aid Co. and other agencies. The cases in which the guns were shipped to Kansas were marked "Bibles" and became known as "Beecher's Bibles". Named for Henry Ward Beecher, a minister active in soliciting aid for Free-Kansas about whom the New York Tribune (Feb. 8, 1856) reported: "He believed that the Sharps

Rifle was a truly moral agency, and that there was more moral power in one of these instruments so far as the slave-holders were concerned than in a "hundred Bibles."

John Brown obtained 200 Sharps carbines from the Massachusetts Committee and used these in 1859 in his daring raid on Harpers Ferry, Virginia.

In the Civil War the Sharps proved effective and approximately 100,000 Sharps arms were used. Colonel Hiram Berdan in 1861 organized two regiments of superior marksmen. They used Sharps arms and acquired a reputation as Sharpshooters. However the term Sharpshooter is not derived from the Sharps arm but has an earlier origin.

The Spencer and the Henry, metallic cartridge and repeating action arms challenged the Sharps as the Civil War drew to a close.

During the 1880s the repeating rifle became increasingly popular.

A. C. Gould in "Modern American Rifles" in 1891 writes: "For several years I thought a single shot Sharps 45 caliber rifle the king of weapons. It had done such fatal work I had a kind of reverence for it . . . the most perfect of all hunting rifles . . . the 1874 model. I could score as many points in a minute as any one with a repeating rifle of the same caliber . . . this is, to some extent true today; but certainly an expert in the use of the repeater can deliver accurate and more rapid fire than one with a single shot rifle."

Sharps Rifle Manufacturing Company was involved in constant and costly litigation due to entangling British Government contracts. In 1874 a settlement was made that involved the sale of the assets of the Sharps Rifle Manufacturing Company.

A new group was organized as the Sharps Rifle Company and incorporated in 1875 with a capital of $100,000. E. G. Westcott was elected president and treasurer, and W. L. Hubbell, secretary.

Bridgeport, Connecticut businessmen led by Mayor Phineas T. Barnum of circus fame, raised forty thousand dollars to induce the Sharps Rifle Company to move to Bridgeport and erect a factory there.

In 1876 Sharps Rifle Company moved to Bridgeport.

In 1881 the company failed.

CHAPTER IV

Christian Sharps in Philadelphia

Christian Sharps is first listed in Philadelphia directories in 1855. His residence is listed at 680 Green Street and his factory at 336 Frankfort Road where he operated as C. Sharps & Co., riflemaker. The year of the publication of a directory was generally about a year after the compilation of the information so that 1855 can be construed as 1854. The manufacture of the Sharps Pistol-Rifle is credited to this period.

It is very light, weighing about five and one half pounds. The barrel is 24½ inches and marked, "C. Sharps and Co., Phila., Pa." Stamped on the right side of the frame is, "C. Sharps Patent '48-'52. It has a cylindrical block, also a Sharps pellet primer and chambered for a metallic cartridge similar to Maynard. The cartridge has a hole in its base which permits the flame from the primer vent to pass through into the powder charge. The Sharps cartridge had a metal tab at its base which stuck upward through a vertical, milled mortise in the breech end of the barrel when the cartridge was loaded into the chamber. This tab is long enough so that it can be grasped by the fingers to remove the empty case from the chamber.

The 1856 Philadelphia directory notes that Sharps had moved his home to 486 Green Street but his shop remained located at 336 Frankfort Road. We also find listed Ira Eddy & Co. as "Manufacturers of Sharps firearms" and located "at the Wire Bridge" a later address of C. Sharps and Co.

Philadelphia Directory listing Christian Sharps:

YEAR	HOME ADDRESS	BUSINESS ADDRESS
1855	680 Green St.	336 Frankford Rd.
1856	486 Green St.	336 Frankford Rd.
1857	486 Green St.	17th and Market St.
1858-60	2322 Green St.	N. 30 near Wire Bridge
1861-65	2216 Green St.	N. 30 near Wire Bridge
1866-68	2216 Green St.	24 St. between Green & Coates St.
1869-70	2206 Green St.	24 St. between Green & Coates St.

The 1857 Philadelphia Directory lists Christian Sharps as living at 486 Green Street, his shop removed to 17th & Market Street and Eddy, Sharps and Co. as manufacturers of Sharps firearms at the "Wire Bridge" The Wire Bridge factory location was at the western end of the 30 Street wire suspension bridge over the Schuylkill River.

Sharps made three types of single shot breech-loading pistols. The first type was a .31 caliber with a five inch barrel and five grooves, right hand twist. It was marked, "Sharps Patent Arms Mfgd. Fairmount Phila., Pa." The other two types were 35 to 38 caliber with 6½ inch barrel, and one type with 8¼ inch barrel. They were rifled six grooves and marked "C. Sharps & Co's. Rifleworks. Phila., Pa."

We find specimens of a six shot percussion revolver, 25 caliber, 6 groove rifling, right twist, and marked on the left side of the barrel, "C. Sharps & Co. Phila., Pa."

It looks like the early Smith & Wesson. Is it possibly a Smith & Wesson evasion that originally was a cartridge revolver and later was converted to percussion is a question.

Specimens of a five shot percussion revolver, caliber 28, marked "Wm. Hankins Phila. Pa.", and similar to the J. P. Lower of Philadelphia revolver, which was a Smith & Wesson infringement, have been found. Did Sharps & Hankins manufacture for J. P. Lower is another question unanswered. John P. Lower later moved from Philadelphia to Denver, Colorado and was an agent for Sharps Rifles.

Christian Sharps obtained patent No. 30765 on November 27, 1860 for a Smith & Wesson evasion by the use of a cap or plate which screwed over the back of the cylinder. No specimens have been found.

The 1858 Philadelphia directory lists Christian Sharps as having moved his residence to 2322 Green Street and his factory to the "Wire Bridge." This listing remained the same for 1859 and 1860. However the 1859 directory notes that C. Sharps & Co. consists of Christian Sharps, Nathan H. Bolles, and Ira B. Eddy.

"Philadelphia and Its Manufacturers" written by Edwin T. Freedley was published in July, 1858 so that the information therein must have been compiled earlier and is presumably predicated upon an interview with Christian Sharps. It notes: "More recently Mr. Sharps applied the principle which distinguishes his rifles for the construction of a new pistol or carbine especially designed for the use of mounted Dragoons . . . it is capable of being fired twice as often as any revolver in a given period of time. The pistol weighs about two and a half pounds; the barrels are six and eight inches long, and throw a half ounce ball effectively one-fourth of a mile. There are about 1,500 pistols now being constructed in the factory. It was recently tested in competition with various other fire-arms, at West Point, by a board of officers appointed by the United States Ordnance Bureau, and struck a target six feet square, at a distance of six hundred yards, twenty out of thirty shots. The same pistol was fired seventy times in seven minutes, priming it three times, every ball striking a target three feet square, at a distance of forty-five feet, with a force sufficient to penetrate eight inches of pine board. Certificates from officers in the army testify to the high estimation in which it is held by the troops that have tried it. During the last year, Mr. Sharps, in association with Nathan H. Bolles and Ira B. Eddy, under the firm-style of C. Sharps & Co., erected a very expensive establishment at the west end of the Wire Bridge near Fairmount. The firm is engaged principally in the construction of Breech-loading and Self-priming pistols, though a large number of rifles are rapidly approaching completion."

The failure of the single-shot lead Sharps on to his 4 barrel repeating pistol. An early advertisement of the 4 barrel states, "Having no revolving cylinder, it shoots past no joint, and consequently, has more penetration than any other firearm of its size."

It was a success. It offered Smith & Wesson competition. It sold at a price. It had hardware store distribution.

Ira B. Eddy first appears in Philadelphia directories in 1856 and is not listed as a resident of Philadelphia in 1858 or thereafter.

Nathan H. Bolles appears in directories in 1858. His residence is 2322 Green Street which is the same address as that of Christian Sharps'. In 1861 Nathan Bolles appears in the directory with a residence at 2216 Green St., the same as Christian Sharps'.

On January 25, 1859 Christian Sharps received a patent for a cartridge repeating pistol. About 60,000 of this first model were manufactured from 1859 until 1867. It was a brass-frame .22 caliber pistol with hard-rubber grips cast in a floral design, and it was stamped "C. Sharps & Co." though the firm changed to Sharps-Hankins in 1862. Handy & Brenner, Hardware wholesales, at 23 N. 5 St. Philadelphia were the sole agents at first though by 1864 Schuyler, Hartley & Graham listed the gun.

It was the first American metal cartridge pistol to attract notice. It was called "The Protector". Four barrels were bored in one solid block. The block was moved forward along a slide to permit loading. There was no extractor. The hammer mechanism was single action and had a ratchet operated nose which moved round through ninety degrees in order to fire the successive barrels. In England it was manufactured by Tipping & Lawden of Birmingham.

Sharps utilized a system of sliding the barrel forward from a fixed breech block. The principle of moving the barrel instead of the breech block was always employed though with variations as to the method. It was the first cartridge derringer.

The derringer was developed by Henry Derringer of Philadelphia as a close range defensive weapon. Small, short-barrelled, and large caliber, it came in with the percussion cap. It was successful, widely imitated, and became the generic term for a small, powerful pistol regardless of ignition.

A multiplicity of systems for breech-loading was contemporaneous with the development of the rim-fire cartridge but claims were limited. Basic features were already in use.

Sharps made 2 claims—a revolving firing pin in the hammer, and catches attached to the breech block for withdrawing the cartridge. The latter feature was not used in production.

It was patent No. 22753 issued on Jan. 25, 1859 and two features shown on the patent drawings which were not used was the ejector and the lever. The ejector had two spring clips fastened on either side to hold the cartridge rims. The lever was a trigger-guard lever to slide the barrels forward and back for loading. An experimental model with the lever feature is known to exist.

The January 1859 patent was reissued on June 18, 1861 and again on Feb. 12, 1867. In 1867 reissue, Sharps writes that, "I am aware that George Leonard, in his patent of Sept. 18, 1849 described a discharger to which such movements could be imparted as to strike, one after another, ordinary caps on a barrel having a number of bores closed at the rear; but I am not aware that the combination of a stationary barrel, having a number of bores open at the rear for the reception of metallic cartridges, with a discharger to which such a motion can be imparted that it will strike one of such cartridges after another was ever known or used prior to the date of my said patent."

This reference to the Leonard patent is most interesting because the Leonard patent was issued three months before Sharps received a patent for a similar percussion pistol on Dec. 18, 1849.

The patent of Dec. 18, 1849 was for a percussion 4 barrel repeating pistol with a revolving striker built into the frame. Sharps never produced this firearm.

A .30 caliber repeating pistol was produced somewhat later and the hard-rubber grips were checkered rather than floral designed.

The .32 caliber repeating pistol manufactured by Sharps & Hankins were chambered for the .32 Long Rimfire with 13 grains of powder while the .30 took the .30 Short Rimfire with 6 grains. The revolving firing-pin in the frame was to help since the charge was more than doubled. This replaced the older mechanism with the revolving firing-pin on the nost of the hammer. Two different versions of the mechanism were used but when both were unsuccessful, it was altered to the hammer mechanism.

In 1862 Sharps formed a partnership with William Hankins as Sharps and Hankins. They manufactured arms for the government during the Civil War. The Philadelphia directory did not note the new firm until the 1864 edition.

The 1858 Philadelphia directory lists William Hankins as a carpenter with his residence at 2322 Green Street, the same residence of both Christian Sharps and Nathan H. Bolles.

In 1862 directory Hankins is listed at 2216 Green Street which is again Sharps' address and he is employed at the rifle factory.

In 1863 directory Sharps and Hankins' partnership is listed.

In 1866 a new plant was built across the river from the Wire Bridge factory, at 24 St. between Green and Coates Street in Philadelphia. The Wire Bridge factory was referred to in Sharps' advertisements as "Fairmount." Both plants operated in 1866, 67 and 68. The Wire Bridge plant was then torn down for the Pennsylvania Railroad expanding yards.

The last directory listing of Sharps & Hankins was in 1867. The 1868 Directory changed Hankins' home address to 2131 Spring Garden and in 1869 his name is no longer listed.

After the Sharps & Hankins partnership dissolution, Sharps continued in business as "Christian Sharps".

Sharps then manufactured a .22 pistol with side-button release for a short time. Then a new model with a release button under the frame but retained the safety interlock of hammer.

Sharps was granted a patent for an improved rifling machine on Dec. 2, 1862.

The first models .22 and .30 pistols are rifled with six grooves, right hand twist. All Sharps and Hankins and all models that followed are rifled with five grooves with left hand twist.

In 1869 the Rollin White patent which protected Smith & Wesson expired. A flood of cheap revolvers followed. Sharps produced a new pistol, the "Bull-dog" or the "2½". It was chambered for the .32 short. It had birdshead grip, shorter barrel of 2½ inches. Otherwise it was almost identical with Sharps & Hankins pistols. The face of the standing breech was recessed for the cartridge heads rather than the barrels; the ejector was discarded; the revolving mechanism is on the hammer. Three models are recognized. One had a screw under frame, a second had a pin on side of frame and the third model had a three-inch barrel and a pin on side of frame.

The new pistol failed to sell. The market had shrunken because the demand had slackened and the supply had increased. Everyone was making cheap revolvers with patent restrictions lifted. Revolvers could be bought as cheaply as Sharps.

B. Kittredge & Co. who bought out the Sharps stock ironically renamed the 'Bulldog', "Sharps Triumph".

In 1871 Sharps moved to Vernon, Connecticut and experimented with trout-breeding. His Philadelphia factory continued to operate until 1874 at which time B. Kittredge & Co. bought out the stock.

Christian Sharps died March 12, 1874, age 64, of tuberculosis, survived by his wife, Sarah Chadwick Sharps, a son Leon Stewart Sharps born in Philadelphia March 10, 1868 and a daughter Satella born in Philadelphia in 1856. The daughter had married Edward T. Waterstone in Vernon, Connecticut on Dec. 23, 1873. Christian Sharps' estate totalled $341.25.

CHAPTER V

The Sharps Rifle

In 1848 Christian Sharps received his basic breech-loading patent. It was a vertical sliding breech-block which closed the rear of the bore when it moved up. A lever opened and closed the block. This lever was pivoted to the receiver and connected to the block through a toggle arrangement.

The unusual in the Sharps model is a gun that conforms to the catalog. The usual in these rugged rifles is the variations in the model.

The metallic cartridge to prevent gas leakage at the breech was not in use then but instead a linen or paper cartridge. The standard military bullet weighed about 475 grains and had a diameter of .56 inch. Bullets were formed in die pressed from cold lead. The powder was black powder. Gas formed from the black powder and resulted in a gummy substance that clogged a gun after a few shots.

The lock mechanism was enclosed in the stock to protect against the gummy substance. Though the gummy substance did form on the breech-block, the lever linkage permitted the block to operate.

Gas leakage not only hindered the operation by the formation of a gummy substance but also wasted powder. If the breech-block would be closely fitted then the leakage would erode the block. Therefore a circular groove was cut into the face of the block and inlaid with a small ring of platinum to resist erosion. In the 1851, 1852 and 1855 models the platinum was used and though platinum was tougher than steel it was not the answer. So another method was tried. The sleeve which formed the lining of the barrel chamber was driven back. The sleeve had to be adjusted with special tools and gas escape persisted.

Hezekiah Conant's patent, of 1856, gas check contributed the answer. It was a closely fitting, sliding, gas check ring set in counterbore in the face of block with a chamber back of it so that the pressure of the explosion forced the ring tightly against the base of the breech and thereby the escape of flame and gas.

From 1859 on, in all percussion models, the ring was lengthened, the rear edge of ring was tapered, and combined with the face-plate so that the explosion expanded the edge of the ring outward against the inside of the counterbore.

Sometimes a linen or paper cartridge was too short or a cartridge forced too far into the chamber. The result was that sharp upper edge of the block closed but failed to cut off the base of the cartridge. To remedy this, cartridges were made with a base of thin gold beaters skin and also the vent opening in the face of the block was put in the center of the counterbore and extended through a hollow cone. The fire from the primer would therefore impinge directly against the skin base of the cartridge. This arrangement made the vent communicating tube longer. To clean the vent tube, a hole was drilled into the tube from the central section and a small headless screw closed the hole. When one wanted to open the screw to clean the vent tube, the screw was gummed with residue and the small screw slot was soon stripped in the attempt to open it. In 1863 a screw with a large filaster head was used.

With "New Model 1859" a broad, shallow channel from top to bottom of the breech-block made the action easier to operate.

Tumblers, bridles, mainsprings and mainspring swivels of 1859 on models of Sharps are interchangeable with Spencer arms Model 1860 and 1865.

In the construction of the model of his repeating rifle invention, Spencer had been assisted by Lawrence and had used parts of the Sharps.

To a great extent, parts of each model from 1851 to 1855 were interchangeable and almost completely interchangeable from 1859 on for percussion actions.

In Models 1851 and 1852 an ordinary spring type barrel band retainer was set into the right-hand side of the forearm in order to hold the arm of the breech-lever pin in its normal position.

Caliber, then was defined in bore size or the number of round lead balls to weigh one pound for each barrel size. Hence the Sharps bore size of 32, 60 and 90 equal caliber .526, .427, and .373. The standard caliber for military models was .52 but are described as "32 bore".

Models 1851 and 1855 had the Maynard type primer. After 1855 the Sharps' pellet primer was used and in 1859 a pellet cut-off was added. This made it possible to load the pellet magazine and keep it in reserve while using regular musket caps. The pellet magazine could be charged with fifty pellets at a time.

Model 1853 has two types of breech-block. The latter type had the improved block with a longer gas check ring and a central primer vent jet and a vent cleanout screw in the side of the block.

In Confederate copies of Sharps many types of blocks were used and sometimes genuine Sharps blocks were captured and used.

21

Many percussion guns were converted into metallic cartridge arms and it was expedient to use but a few new parts.

A new type of block containing a firing pin, the hammer was modified, and an extractor was added but the other parts were those used in the vertical block percussion model.

The extractor was pivoted on the breech lever pin along with the lever itself.

The firing pin had an odd "U" shape and therefore failed to transmit to the cartridge primer the full force of the hammer impact.

The 1869 report of the Chief of Ordnance states, "The altered Sharps' carbines give great satisfaction, particularly in the ammunition, which is the same as the breech-loading musket ammunition; it is decidely superior to the Spencer carbine."

In 1871 at the Springfield Armory the government made one thousand "Sharps Conversion of the Springfield Musket". It used a new breech action and frame based on the regular Sharps action, but modified to handle a rimfire cartridge combined with the Springfield musket barrel reduced to 50 caliber and using the Springfield fore-stock, bands, butt stock and butt plate. This arm was used for experimental trial in the field and submitted to the Ordnance Board of 1872.

Harpers Weekly in the issue of October 13, 1877 reported: "The Sharps Rifle Company at Bridgeport is filling a large order for their new model breech-loaders for the Chinese government. Each rifle is marked 'Old Reliable' in Chinese characters."

Old percussion parts were used until late in 1877 a completely different gun, the Borchardt, was introduced. Hugo Borchardt, a German immigrant, was an inventor and later responsible for the Luger pistol. He had worked for several companies including Winchester when in 1875 he became superintendent of Sharps Rifle Co. In 1877 the Sharps-Borchardt model was introduced. It was a radical and premature model—an excellent single shot action with coil springs and no outside hammer.

A weakness which may have affected U.S. Army acceptance was the failure of the firing pin to retract before the block started to drop upon opening. After the firing pin punctured the cartridge primer, it was difficult to open the action.

The Borchardt was made from 1877 to 1881—a very short time but it was adopted by the National Guard of North Carolina and Michigan as the official firearm.

All Borchardts had round barrels except the Sporting Model 1878 and the Express Model 1878. The military Sharps-Borchardt was made only in 45/70 government caliber with 32" round barrels.

E. S. Farrow, U.S. Military Academy Instructor, in "American Small Arms" (1904) wrote about the Sharps-Borchardt rifle, "Perhaps this was the most remarkable rifle of its time; it certainly did more to popularize rifles than any other invention that had preceded it."

MODEL	BARREL	OVERALL	PRIMER	MARKINGS & REMARKS
1851 carbine	21 5/8	37 3/8	Maynard	Bbl: "U.S., S.K. & P." Tang: "Co Sharps Patent 1848". Numbers used consecutively until 1864 when numbers prefixed by "C".
1852 carbine	21 3/4	37 3/8	Sharps pellet without cut-off	Bbl: "U.S., S.K. & P." or "Sharps Rifle Manufg. Co. Hartford, Conn" U.S. Army bought 200, Britain bought a few.
1853 carbine	21 3/4	37 3/4	Pellet without cut-off	These were the model captured from John Brown at Harpers Ferry in 1859. Bbl: "Sharps Rifle Manufg. Co. Hartford, Conn."
1855 rifle	28 1/4	44 1/4	Maynard	In 1855 U.S. Army bought 400. Bbl: "Sharps Rifle Manufg. Co. Conn." or "U.S., J.H. & P."
carbine	21 3/4	37 3/4		
1855 British	18	34	Maynard	6000 mfgd. Marked with Broad Arrow, Crown V.R. Issued to British Cavalry in 1857.
	21	34		
1859 carbine	21 5/8	38 5/8	Pellet	First of Straight block model; all previous models were Slanting block. "Sharps Rifle Manufg. Co."
1859 carbine	22	39 1/8	Primer with Lawrence cut-off	Bbl: "New Model 1859"
rifle	30	47		
rifle musket	36	53		
1863 carbine	22	39 1/8	Lawrence cut-off	Bbl: "New Model 1863"
rifle	30	47		
Confederate Copy	21 5/8	38 1/2	none	Mfgd. with captured parts. Some marked, "S. G. Robinson Arms Manufactory, Richmond, Va."

***All these models have nominal caliber .52; all are percussion ignition.

****Sharps rifles showed little uniformity in the models except for the military models. These eight percussion models outlined above were made in quantity and therefore had standard actions. Varied sporting rifles were also produced and though they had a combination of style features yet. For Example: the barrel shape or the engraving may differ yet the models had the same action parts as the military models that were current. Repairs or replacements also resulted in variations so that it is oftimes difficult to determine a model. The test of a model is the overall evaluation of a combination of parts.

1851 Box Lock Hunting Rifle Cal .44 Sharps linen, 36 Sharps linen (linen and a charge of powder glued to rear end of conical bullet) bbl: 27″ oct. Overall: 44½″ Weighs: 9¾ lbs. bbl. marked, "Robbins & Lawrence, Windsor, Vt." Half-stocked, without patch-box, plain cast-steel bbl; without rod or guard, plain breech, black walnut stock, Maynard lock and primer.
Carbine.
Cal .52 Sharps linen. 44 Sharps linen. Bbl. 23″ rd. marked "C. Sharps, Pat. 1848." has front sight cover and a tang peep sight.
Rifle.
Cal. 36 Sharps linen bbl. 28″ oct.

1852 Slanting Breech. Cal. 44, 36, and 52 Sharps linen. Bbl. 26″ oct. marked: "Sharps Rifle Manufg. Co., Hartford, Conn." Lawrence pellet primer, Overall: 42½″ rifled with 8 grooves. Top of receiver tang marked, "C. Sharps, Pat. 1848".
Carbine.
Cal. 52 Sharps. Bbl. 21½″, 6 grooves. 37¾″ overall. 7¼ lb. weight.

1855 Slanting Breech Carbine
Cal. 52 Sharps linen. Maynard 1855 primer. Mfgd. for British Government 6000 mfgd. 3,000 had 18″ bbl.; 3,000 had 21″ bbl. No engraving except Crown and V.R.

1856 These models were manufactured by Sharps Rifle Manufacturing Co. in 1856 with the the following designations:
Army Rifle (self-cocking)
Carbine
Half-engraved rifle, octagon bbl: 60 bore
Extra-fine engraved, octagon bbl; 60 bore
Shotgun
Octagon Rifle, 34″ barrel
English Carbine, Maynard primer
Octagon rifle, 32 bore, double trigger.

1857 Percussion Rifle.

1859 Percussion Carbine. Cal. 52 Sharps linen BBl. 22″ Lockplate marked, "C. Sharps Pat. Oct. 5, 1852 "R. S. Lawrence, patented Feb. 15, 1859." Few manufactured with coffee mill in stock, to enable soldiers to grind coffee bean on the field.

1859 New Model Cal. 52 Sharps linen. Bbl. marked, "New Model 1859"
Military Rifle Cal. 52 Sharps linen, bbl; 30″ Overall 47″ U. S. Army in 1862 bought about 2,000.

1862 Sharps & Hankins Carbine
Military Rifle.

1863 New Model Carbine; cal. 52 Sharps linen. bbl. marked, "New Model 1863"
Military Rifle, 6,000 bought by U.S. in 1865

1867 Commercial Conversion of Military Rifle cal. 52/70 Sharps rimfire 50/67/487 Sharps though the semi-conical ball diameter was .52 and the bbl. .52 cal. Bbl: 30 inches. Overall 46¾″.
Conversion commercial of Carbine.
Cal. 52 sharps special rimfire cartridge. Used old perc. gun parts.

1868 Sharps & Hankins. Rimfire Sporting Carbine cal. 45 S.&H. rimfire bbl: 22″. Model in 1878 was altered for 45 Colt cartridge.

1868 Sporting Rifle
Cal. 40/50; 40/70; 44/77 all Sharps bottleneck, also 50/70 Gov't.

1869 Cartridge Carbine. Cal. 50 reduced from 52 cal. because the bbls. were relined. The bbls. were bored out, a liner inserted, and then rifled. The lining job was done at Springfield Armory. Bbl: 22″ Overall: 39″ Weight 9 lbs. 9 oz. These were 31,098 Civil War guns altered between Feb. 1868 and Oct., 1869 by Sharps Rifle Manufacturing Co. for the government according to the contract Nov. 2, 1867. A new breech block replaced the percussion type.

1869 Military Rifle. cal. 50/70 Govt. centerfire. 1086 Civil War rifles were altered during 1869. The barrels were relined at Springfield Armory. The breechloaders were altered at Sharps factory. 3 bands held the stock to the barrel.

1871 Military Rifle cal. 50/70 gov't. bbl: 32½″. Alteration of 1000 percussion model and putting on Model 1868 Springfield barrels. 2 bands. Issued as regular infantry in 1871 in compliance with recommendation of 1870 Ordnance board at St. Louis.

1873 Creedmoor Rifle—side-hammer. Cal. 44 only and ranging from 44/90 through 44/100 and 44/105. BBL: 30, 32 full-oct; 32 full-oct & half-oct. single triggers, pistol grips mostly for various 44 cal. bottlenecks. Sometimes a 45 cal. has appeared.

Company reorganized as SHARPS RIFLE CO.

Model 1874—Sporting Rifle. Introduced in 1876. Cal: 40/50; 40/70 Sharps bottleneck, 44/77 Sharps bottleneck, 44/90 Sharps bottleneck, 45/70 gov't., 45/90 Sharps straight, 50/70 gov't., 50/90 Sharps straight. Bbl: 29″ & 30″ octagon-single trigger.

Business Rifle. Model 1874. introduced in 1875. Cal. 40/70 Sharps bottleneck, 45/-70 gov't.

Bbl: 28 round; double triggers.

Hunters Rifle, Model 1874. Introduced in 1875. Cal. 40/50, 40/70 Sharps bottleneck, 45/70 gov't., 45/90 Sharps straight. Bbl: 26, 28, 30 round. By 1878 this model only in cal. 40/50 Sharps and Bbl: 26″ round.

1874 Long Range Creedmoor No. 1 Used Model 1874 action, cal. 44/105/520 Sharps bottleneck bbl: 34″ pistol grip-DeLuxe model of Creedmoor 1, 2, 3. Discontinued 1876.

Long Range Creedmoor no. 2—less expensive model of no. 1 discontinued 1876.

Long Range Creedmoor no. 3—least expensive model. Discontinued 1876.

1875 Mid-Range no. 1 Target. Used Model 1874 action. Cal. 44/70/330 Sharps bottleneck. bbl. 30″ oct. or half-oct. deluxe model of Mid-Range no's. 1, 2, 3.

Mid-Range no. 2 Target.—less expensive model of no. 1 but could be chambered for heavier cartridges at extra cost of $1. By 1878 the powder charge had been reduced to 44/50/265.

Mid-Range no. 3 Target. Least expensive of three models. Discontinued 1877.

1875 Rifle. Small number mfgd. for a few months and few carried name "Freund". An article on this model is featured in Forest & Stream Jan. 10, 1884.

1876 Sporting Rifle

1877 Long Range Creedmoor made in 3 grades No. 1, 2 & 3. Cal. 45 Sharps straight. Smaller lockplate, different hammer than model 1874 type. Discontinued 1878.

1878 Military Borchardt. Cal. 45/70 gov't; 45/75/420 Sharps straight. BBl: "Old Reliable" "Sharps Rifle Co., Bridgeport, Conn." Frame: "Borchardt's Pat. Sharps Rifle Co., Bridgeport, Conn."

BBl: 32″ round. Available for double-set triggers. Adopted by Michigan and North Carolina National Guard. Discontinued 1881.

Military Carbine. Cal. 45/70 gov't; 45/75/420 Sharps. Bbl. 24″. Disc. 1881.

Sharps-Borchardt cal. 45 bbl. 32—see catalog description. Disc. 1881.

Mid-Range: cal. 40/70 Sharps str. bbl: 30″. Disc. 1881. In standard grade but available in extra-fancy stock and engraving.

Long-Range: cal. 45/90. DeLuxe models to order. Disc. 1881.

1879 Hunters Rifle. cal. 40/50 & 40/70. bbl. 28″ rd. or oct. Discontinued 1881.

Business Rifle 40/70 & 40/90 Sharps bottleneck. bbl: 28″ oct. Disc. 1881.

Sporting Rifle cal. 40/70; 45/100 Sharps; bbl: 30 rd. or oct. Disc. 1881.

Express Rifle cal. 45 Sharps straight; bbl: 26″ oct. pistol grip. Disc. 1881.

Short-Range Rifle cal. 40/50 Sharps str. 40/70 disc. 1881.

Officers Military Rifle. cal. 45/70 gov't; 45/75/420 Sharps. Disc. 1881.

Borchardt: Round barrels regularly used in military rifle, carbine, Hunters, Business; Short Range; Mid Range, and Long Range. Octagonal barrels or round barrels used in Sporting Rifle, Model 1878 and octagonal barrel 26 inches in Express Rifle. The better grades had fancy walnut panels set into milled recesses. The Borchardt was modernized for modern cartridges by rebushing the firing pin-hole.

* Rollin White invented the self-cocking device used on a few guns. C. Sharps & Co., Pa. Officer's & Model (Pistol-Rifle) cal. 40; 24½ inch barrel; Left side of receiver marked, "C. Sharps & Co., Philada, Pa." Sharps & Hankins, Philadelphia.

Navy Carbine cal. 54; 23 5/8 inch barrel; Breech action—the barrel slid forward to open the breech for loading. Heavy leather covering on barrel to protect barrel from salt water rusting.

Rifle cal. 52 marked "Sharps Patent 1859. Sharps & Hankins, Philada."

Army Rifle cal. 54; 32½ inch tapering barrel; marked, "Sharps and Hankins, Philada. Sharps Patent. 1859."

Carbine: cal. 50; bbl: 24″. rim-fire cart. Used during Civil War and afterwards issued to Indians for sporting purposes.

SHARPS 4 Barreled Pistols

There were over 150,000 Sharps 4 barreled pistols manufactured. They were made in 3 calibers: 22, 30 and 32, and in 15 models, 4 models in cal. 22; 3 models in cal. 30; and 8 models in cal. 32.

22 Caliber	Distance frame to muzzle	Grips	Rifling
Model 1	1/8 inch	Rubber Floral	6 Right Hand Twist
2	½	Wood	5 Left Hand Twist
3	¼	Wood	5 L. H. Twist
4	¼	Wood	5 L. H. Twist
30 caliber			
Model 1.	5/8 inch	Checkered rubber	6 R.H.T.
2.	¾ inch	Wood	5 L.H.T.
3.	¾ inch	Wood	5 L.H.T.

32 caliber	Details
Model 1	small firing pin, firing mechanism in frame
2	large firing pin, firing mechanism in frame
3	firing mechanism on the hammer
4	firing mechanism on the hammer, conventional latch
5	revolving mechanism on hammer
Bulldog 6	2½ inch barrel; screw under frame
7	2½ inch barrel; pin on side of frame
8	3 in barrel; pin on side of frame

SHARPS PISTOLS

1856 Single shot, breech-loading pistols. cal. 31, 5 inch barrel, 5 grooves, right hand twist. Marked, "Sharps Patent Arms, Mfgd. Fairmount Phila. Pa." Possibly mfgd. by Ira Eddy.

1857 6 Shot Percussion Revolver. cal. 25, 6 groove right hand twist, marked on left side of barrel, "C. Sharps & Co. Phila Pa." Very rare. Looks exactly like early model Smith & Wesson except for having a percussion cylinder.

Colt's patents extension expired February 25, 1857 and thereafter percussion revolver was permissable. This revolver is not patened and possibly because it does not offer patenable attributes.

1858 Single Shot, breech-loading pistol cal. 35 to cal. 38, 6½ inch barrel, marked, "C. Sharps & Co.'s Rifleworks Phila, Pa." 6 grooves, right hand twist.

SHARPS METALLIC CARTRIDGE. The first metallic cartridge rifle was the Model 1866. It was chambered for .54 rim-fire cartridge similar to Spencer repeating rifle. Many were chambered for the .50-70 army cartridge. Most of the metallic ammunition had paper-patched bullets.

Caliber	Powder Grains*	Bullet Grains*			
40	50	246	44	90	450
40	50	238	44	90	500
40	50	265	44	100	277
40	45	265	44	105	520
40	70	265	45	70	400
40	70	285	45	70	420
40	70	330	45	100	550
40	70	370	45	100	550
40	65	330	45	100	550
40	90	370	45	90	500
40	100	190	45	100	500
44	70	312	45	110	293
44	70	380	50	70	425
44	70	422	50	70	457
44	75	297	50	70	500
44	75	380	50	110	335
44	75	405	50	170	700

ORDNANCE PURCHASED JAN. 1, 1861, TO JUNE 30, 1866

In addition government manufactured 801,997 Springfield rifled muskets, 50,617,898 cartridges for carbines, 424,441,565 musket cartridges, cal. 57,758; 221,571,978 other musket cartridges; 64,385,403 pistol cartridges; 327,192,861 percussion caps; 10,281,305 friction primers.
The regulation infantry arm was the .58 calibre Springfield muzzle-loading rifled musket.

CARBINES

Ball	1,002
Ballard	1,509
Burnside	55,567
Cosmopolitan	9,342
Gallagher	22,728
Gibbs	1,052
Hall	3,520
Joslyn	11,261
Lindner	892
Merrill	14,495
Maynard	20,202
Palmer	1,001
Remington	20,000
Sharps	80,512
Smith	30,062
Spencer	94,196
Starr	25,603
Warner	4,001
Wesson	151
French carbines	200
Foreign carbines	10,051
Musketoons	587

PISTOLS

Allen	536
Adam	415
Beall	2,814
Colt army	129,730
Colt navy	17,010
Joslyn	1,100
Perrin	200
Penntengil	2,001
LeFaucheux	12,374
Remington army	125,314
Remington navy	4,901
Raphael	978
Savage	11,284
Starr	47,952
Roger & Spencer	5,000
Whitney	11,214
foreign pistols	100
horse pistols	200
signal pistols	348

APPENDAGES

ball screws	10,876
cones	130,952
screw-drivers	93,332
spring fuses	2,832
swages	4,250
tompions	3,559
wipers	31,704
Sharps primers	2,557,574

CARTRIDGES

Ballard	3,527,450
Burnside	21,819,200
Cosmopolitan	6,300,000
Gallagher	8,294,023
Greene	173,760
Henry	4,610,400
Joslyn	515,416
Lindner	100,000
Maynard	2,157,000
Merrill	5,502,750
Remington	4,257,000
Sharps	16,306,508
Sharps & Hankins	1,001,000
Smith	13,861,500
Spencer	58,238,924
Starr	6,860,000
Warner	1,028,000
rifle .58	46,409,514
Wesson	254,000
buck & ball	6,021,220
LeFaucheux	842,880
round ball	2,735,180
blank	2,047,011
carbine	2,852,000
pistol	26,225,930
Gardener shell	10,000

MUSKETS & RIFLES

Springfield rifle musket caliber .58	670,617
Lindsay double shot muskets	1,000
Ballards rifles	35
Colt's revolving rifles	4,612
Greene's rifles	900
H...enry rifles	1,731
Merrill's rifles	583
Sharps rifles	9,141
Spencer rifles	12,471
Hall rifles	1,575
Harper Ferry rifles	22,793
Caliber .69 rifles	1,832
Enfield, caliber .577, triangle bay.	428,292
Enfield, caliber .577 sword bay.	8,034
Boker rifle	162,533
Boker rifle, sword bay.	25,000
French rifles	44,250
Belgian rifle	57,467

Austrian rifle 226,294
Prussian rifle 59,918
Jager rifle 29850
Suhl rifle 1,673
Tower rifle 4,182
Garibaldi rifle 5,995
Prussian Smoothbore musket 81,652
foreign smoothbore musket..29,201
American smoothbore musket..2,181
rifles, various kinds 641

SHARPS RIFLE MANUFACTURING CO.

1848—Christian Sharps received basic patent and contracted the manufacturing of the Sharps rifle

1851—Sharps Rifle Manufacturing Co. organized in Hartford, Conn.

1853—R. S. Lawrence assumes management of Sharps Rifle Manufacturing Co. Christian Sharps severs connection beyond royalty rights and moves to Philadelphia.

1874—Sharps Rifle Manufacturing Co. reorganized as Sharps Rifle Co.

1875—Nelson King, inventor Winchester loading improvement, was Superintendent.

1876—Plant moved from Hartford to Bridgeport, Conn.

1881—Sharps Rifle Co. discontinued production.

CHRISTIAN SHARPS

1853—C. Sharps left Hartford and moved to Philadelphia.

1855—C. Sharps operated as C. Sharps & Co.

1857—C. Sharps operated as Eddy, Sharps & Co.

1858—C. Sharps & Co. was now a partnership of C. Sharps with Nathan H. Bolles & Ira B. Eddy.

1862—Sharps & Hankins. A partnership of C. Sharps with William Hankins, an associate since 1858.

1871—C. Sharps left Philadelphia and moved to Vernon, Conn. where he resided until his death in 1874.

Officers and Directors of Sharps Rifle Manufacturing Company

1851: Pres. John C. Palmer Sect'y: Daniel Penfield Treas: John C. Palmer. Directors: M. W. Chapin, James Goodwin, S. E. Robbins, Wm. T. Lee.

1852: Pres: John C. Palmer: Sect'y: Daniel Penfield: Treas: John C. Palmer. Directors: M. W. Chapin, James Goodwin, S. E. Robbins, Thos. Belknap.

1853: Pres: John C. Palmer: Sect'y: E. Thos. Lobdell: Treas: John C. Palmer. Directors: M. W. Chapin, James Goodwin, Thos. Belknap, Wm. T. Lee, C. H. Northram, H. Huntington.

1854: Pres: John C. Palmer: Sect'y: E. Thos. Lobdell: Treas: John C. Palmer. Directors: Wm. Jarvis added to directors listed in 1853.***—SEE NOTE:

1855: Pres: John C. Palmer: Sect'y: E. Thos. Lobdell: Treas: John C. Palmer. Directors: David Clark replaced Wm. T. Lee, other directors the same.

1856: Pres: R. L. Baker: Sect'y: E. Thos. Lobdell: Treas: John C. Palmer. Directors: R. L. Baker, M. W. Chapin, James Goodwin, Thos. Belknap, Wm. Jarvis, Thos. Smith, John Seymore, Elisha Colt, W. J. Hamersley.

1857: Pres: R. L. Baker: Sect'y: Samuel H. Green. Treas: John C. Palmer. Directors: S. C. Preston, W. J. Babcock and David Clark replaced Seymore, Colt and Hamersley.

1858: Pres. John C. Palmer: Sect'y: Samuel H. Green. Treas: John C. Palmer. Directors: R. L. Baker out and H. Huntington replaced W. J. Babcock.

1859: Pres: John C. Palmer: Sect'y: Samuel H. Green. Treas: John C. Palmer. Directors: S. C. Preston—unchanged.

1860: Pres: John C. Palmer: Sect'y: Samuel H. Green. Treas: John C. Palmer. Directors: Unchanged.

1861: Pres: John C. Palmer: Sect'y: Samuel H. Green. Treas: John C. Palmer. Directors. D. W. Pardee replaced Wm. Jarvis.

1862: Pres: John C. Palmer: Sect'y: Samuel H. Green. Treas: John C. Palmer. Directors: James Goodwin, Thos. Belknap; David Clark, H. Huntington, D. W. Pardee, S. Tudor Woolcott.

1863: Pres: John C. Palmer: Sect'y: Samuel H. Green. Treas: John C. Palmer. Directors: Unchanged.

1864: Pres: John C. Palmer: Sect'y: Samuel H. Green. Treas: John C. Palmer. Directors: Thos. Smith replaced H. Huntington.

1865: Pres: John C. Palmer: Sect'y & Treas: Unchanged. Directors: James Goodwin, M. W. Chapin, S. Tudor Woolcott, Thos. Smith, Guy R. Phelps, Emerson Gaylord.

1866: Pres: James T. Ames: Sect'y & Treas: Unchanged. Directors: Phelps replaced by James T. Ames and added: David Clark, John B. Taft, Chas. H. Sage, Frank W. Burr, and James P. Taylor.

1867: Pres: James T. Ames: Sect'y & Treas: Unchanged: Directors. David Clark, John B. Taft, Frank W. Burr, James B. Taylor replaced by David Hoadley and Geo. H. Penfield.

1868: Pres: James T. Ames: Sect'y & Treas: Unchanged Directors: Nathan Waterman added and Hoadley and Penfield out.

1870: Pres: Thos Belknap: Sect'y Samuel H. Green. Treas: Asa S. Porter. Directors: Thos. Belknap, John C. Palmer, Nathan Waterman, L. M. Hotchkiss, Francis W. Burr, S. T. Woolcott, Asa S. Porter.

1871: Pres: Thos. Belknap: Sect'y & Treas: Unchanged: Directors: Geo. S. Gilman replaced Hotchkiss.

1872: Pres: Thos. Belknap: Sect'y & Treas: Unchanged: Directors: Frederick S. Brown and Samuel Elmore added.

1873: Pres: Thos. Belknap: Sect'y: Samuel H. Green Treas: George F. Hills. Directors: John C. Palmer out and Geo. F. Hills added.

NOTE: 1854—William Jarvis was possibly Samuel Colt's brother-in-law who became president of Colt's in 1865.

SHARPS' BREECH-LOADING PATENT RIFLE.---Fig 1.

This Rifle is the invention of Mr. Christian Sharps, now of Mill Creek, Pa. It was patented in 1848. The simplicity of its construction, will be apparent by the following description

Fig 1 is a side view showing the cap box open. Fig 2, is a section showing the interior of the cap box. Fig. 3 is a top or plan view The same letters refer to like parts. The engravings represent the barrel and the butt broken off, (as every body understands such parts) in order to present enlarged and clearer views. A represents the wooden stock. T is the barrel; B is the nipple or priming chamber communicating by a small orifice with the charge in the barrel, N, is the hammer. The charge is put in at the breech, and the breech itself is a moveable steel back, J, that is pushed up like a wedge to back the charge in the barrel, and then drawn down to allow another charge to be inserted. There is therefore a strong metal chamber behind the butt of the barrel, and a broad shot in it, in which the moveable steel breech, T, is thrust

Fig 2.

up and down. This sliding breech is secured by a swivel pivot, O, which moves the breech up and down for the purpose stated, by being operated by the handle, D, which moves on a centre pin, C, thus allowing said handle to be drawn inwards to the butt (fig. 1) of the stock, when the breech is to be raised and pushed outwards (fig. 2) for the breech to be lowered for charging. To charge, the handle D is pushed forward, as represented in fig. 2, when the ball, S, is thrust along the groove, R, into the chamber of the barrel, when the handle, D, is drawn back, as in fig. 1, the sliding steel breech, J, is pushed up, wedging behind the charge, and it is then loaded ready for firing. It is designed for caps, and is self-capping. This is done by the caps, E, being set on spurs of a small moveable wheel, F, in the cap-box, P, as shown in fig. 1. This wheel is taken out, armed around with caps, and set on to two small catches, M, which project out from each side of a barrel spring box, L. The spring is not shown, but it will be understood

to be attached to the box, L, inside, and to its screw arbor. The object of this barrel spring is to turn round the wheel, F with the caps on it, towards the priming box, B. At H is a small iron plate, and behind it is a narrow channel, into which the caps are carried inwards, stripped off, one by one, as they pass through the channel behind the plate, H, and the one pushes the other forward above the small nipple opening, when the nipple, X, when rising, (as it forms part of the sliding breech) catches the cap, and thus caps itself. The wheel moves round one cap every shot, by one being exploded to make way for another to pass into the said channel. The wheel may be capped for 50 rounds. In fig. 2, in the inside of the spring barrel box, P, attached to the barrel box, L, there is a catch, G, shaped like an angular lever. This catch is for the purpose of holding the barrel box, under the plate, H, after it is wound up, to take off the wheel, cap it, and put it on again. It is then set free for the wheel to move gradually round. K is the lid of the cap box. This gun can be capped like another, without the self-capping

Fig. 3.

auxiliary action, and presents a breech-loading rifle of singularly simple construction —
This rifle can be loaded and fired nine times in one minute. Its accuracy is equal to the common rifle. The picket, or patched ball can be used. It can carry half a mile with safety, and in one instance it was fired nine times in one minute and all the balls were placed within a circle of six inches diameter, at forty yards distance. Mr. Albert S. Nippes, is now making about 700 of them of the very best materials, and of superior workmanship. Orders addressed, (p p) to Mr Nippes, Mill Creek, Manyunck Post Office, Philadelphia Co., Pa., will meet with prompt attention.

30

IMPROVEMENT IN RIFLES.

This is an improvement in Rifles, combining Sharp's Patent Loading Breech, and Dr. Maynard's Patent Self-Priming Rifles. In No. 25 of our last volume we published an illustrated description of Sharp's Rifle, and we would refer our readers to that for an explanation of the manner by which this rifle is loaded at the breech.

The accompanying engraving only illustrates the improved mode of priming, which is the invention of Dr. Maynard, of Washington. The engraving is a side view, with the priming box open; no caps are used; the priming is a patent preparation of percussion paper made into a coiled ribbon, represented by D, and placed in the inside of a small box, which is now represented as being open. F shows the edge of the lid; A is the hammer; E is the nipple of the priming orifice. It will be observed that the strip of priming ribbon passes over the top of the nipple. It will also be noticed that there is a notch in the end of

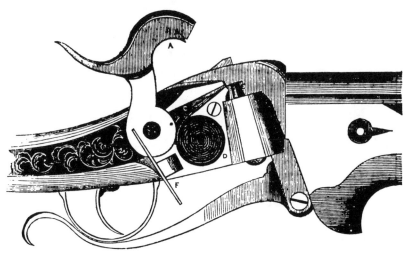

the hammer, A; this cuts off the strip of ribbon as the hammer is coming down on the nipple, and when the hammer strikes the prepared paper, it being percussive, the powder is ignited, and the gun discharged. The question may now be asked, " how is the paper fed over the nipple for a new priming, after having been cut off by the hammer?" This is done by a small flat steel spring, B, secured on the periphery of the ring of the hammer joint. When the hammer is drawn back, it will be observed that the flat spring, B, is moved forward, pushing the priming strip over the orifice of the nipple for the next discharge. When the hammer, A, falls down on the nipple, it will be observed, the spring, B, is drawn back for a new feed of the paper. This would draw back some of the paper, were it not for another small stationary flat spring, C, which holds the paper so as to allow it to be fed only up and along the metal incline to cover the nipple. This is the most ingenious, simple, and effective method of priming firearms ever discovered. Albert S. Nippes & Co. have the exclusive right to apply Dr. Maynard's Primer to Sharp's Rifle, with the exception of the U. S. Government privilege to the same. These rifles, thus improved, are manufactured and sold by Butterfield & Nippes, Kensington, Philadelphia. Capt. Tansil, of the U. S. Marine Corps, and a board of Ordnance officers, have reported in favor of the warlike instrument. A ball was fired by it along the surface of the Potomac, and it was loaded and fired again so quick that the two balls were seen skipping along the surface of the water at one time, a good evidence of the speed whereby it can be loaded.

☞ The following Official reports and disinterested Recommendations are submitted, in confirmation of the superiority of our arms over others, to which an indefinite number might be added.

REPORT

OF THE

BOARD OF ORDNANCE OFFICERS,

On Patent Small Arms other than Repeating Pistols.

SHARPS' RIFLE AND MUSKET.

WASHINGTON, D. C., Nov. 27, 1850.

This is an arm loading at the breech, which is opened or closed by a vertical slide or shear cutting off the end of the cartridge. This arm has withstood all the trials the Board has considered necessary to make with it. It has fired several hundred times without cleaning, during which the movements of its machinery were not obstructed. The arm is loaded with great ease and rapidity by using a simply prepared cartridge which Mr. Sharps has arranged ; and also the ordinary rifle and musket ammunition with its percussion caps can be used with facility.

The penetration, range and accuracy of fire from the rifle thus arranged, with the cartridge and conical ball thus prepared for it, were superior to that of any other breech loading piece offered to the Board. With Maynard's primer, (which, as well as the cap may be used,) this arm was fired ten times per minute, and when discharged over the water, a second charge was fired before the ricochet of the first had ceased.

From the observations of the use of this Rifle, the Board are of the opinion that it is superior to any of the other arms loading at the breech, and think it would be well to have further trials made, and to put some of them into the hands of troops to determine whether they are suitable to the military service.

All of which is respectfully submitted.

R. L. BAKER,
MAJOR AND BREVET LIEUTENANT COLONEL, President of the Board.
A. MORDECAI,
CAPTAIN ORDNANCE, BREVET MAJOR.
BENJ. HUGER,
CAPTAIN, BREVET COLONEL.
W. A. THORNTON,
CAPTAIN OF ORDNANCE AND BREVET MAJOR.
G. H. TALCOTT,
CAPTAIN ORDNANCE AND BREVET LIEUTENANT COLONEL.

J. L. RENO,
SECOND LIEUTENANT, BREVET CAPTAIN, Recorder of Board.

Sir:—I herewith submit for your consideration, the result of the trials made as to the comparative merits of Sharps' improved rifle and the rifle musket now in use in the Marine corps.

I selected for the trial a recruit uninstructed in the manual of either, and the following table is the result of the firing:

MUSKET.		SHARPS' RIFLE.	
Number of rounds fired at 100 yds.,	30	Number of rounds fired at 100 yds.,	40
Hit,	13	Hit,	35
Missed,	17	Missed,	5
Number of rounds fired at 200 yds.,	5	Number of rounds fired at 200 yds.,	5
Hit,	4	Hit,	4
Missed,	1	Missed,	1
Number of rounds fired at 300 yds.,	15	Number of rounds fired at 300 yds.,	15
Hit,	3	Hit,	9
Missed,	12	Missed,	6
Number of rounds fired at 450 yds.,	10	Number of rounds fired at 450 yds.,	7
Hit,	00	Hit,	5
Missed,	10	Missed,	2
Recapitulation.		*Recapitulation.*	
Total number of rounds,	60	Total number of rounds,	67
Hit,	20	Hit,	53
Missed,	40	Missed,	14

After Sharps' arm had been fired 100 times and the musket 50 times, I placed the latter in the hands of a recruit who had never loaded a musket, and directed him to commence firing. During two minutes he fired four times and hit the target once. With Sharps' in the same time and under the same circumstances, he fired nine times and hit the target eight, showing a great superiority of Sharps' rifle over the musket for precision, and fully equal in point of range. The difference in rapidity of loading and firing was vastly in favor of Sharps' rifle, being as 4 or 6 to 1—and I also noticed what seemed to me to be a fact of great importance in actual service, that while the marine who exercised the musket was giving unremitted observation to the arm during the process of loading, and remained in a fixed position, the operator having Sharps' rifle could load instantly at a walk or run, keeping his eye on other objects, the arm not requiring the least observation except at the instant of firing. I have seen it stated that celerity of loading and firing might be found objectionable, as the soldier would too soon expend his ammunition. I had this matter in consideration during the trials, and I am fully convinced that there is no force to such an objection. The soldier in battle possessed of a gun that can be instantly reloaded, keeping his eye on the foe, confident of his power and strength (that he is always ready,) naturally inspires him with courage and self-possession, which is valuable to the soldier.

On the other hand, armed with the muzzle-loading rifle, the soldier's severest trial occurs after he has discharged his piece and during the interval of reloading; hence it is, after an engagement, so many arms are found disabled by the insertion of the ball below the powder, or double or treble loading.

I can see no reason to justify the idea that a soldier, qualified with an arm possessing great celerity of fire, is likely to waste his ammunition at the first sight of a distant enemy, but on the contrary, in my opinion, the soldier would carefully reserve his strength until he came to the thickest of the fight.

It seems to me that the efficiency of the soldier can in no wise be disparaged by the fact that he has no time or observation comparatively to bestow in loading his weapon.

On my return from practice the arms were put away without cleaning for one week, when both were examined; and while the present service musket needed the attention of the armorer at the armory, and much time to put it in order, Sharps' rifle was easily cleaned by myself at the office.

Sharps' arm is simple in its construction, and can be handled by the most inexperienced soldier.

The use of Sharps' carbine for the last seven years in the army has shown its efficiency as a service arm in the field, sufficiently to authorize its adoption in that branch of the service, and there is no other test but field service which would, in my opinion, warrant the adoption of any arm.

The objections that have been heretofore made to this gun of escapement of gas at the breech, waste of powder by the cut-off, difficulty of inserting the cartridge without bursting it, paper left behind in the chamber, have all been obviated.

I feel authorized, in view of all the facts connected with this arm in the service, most respectfully to recommend its adoption to the marine corps, believing, as I do, that such action on the part of the government will increase the efficiency of that force more than double its present power.   Respectfully,
                                                    J. GREEN,
                                        1ST LIEUTENANT U. S. MARINES.

To COL. JOHN HARRIS,
    COMMANDANT MARINE CORPS.

SHARPS' CARBINES.

Official Certificates of their value by Officers of the Army.

NEW YORK ARSENAL, April 10th, 1858.

SIR:—I have the honor herewith to enclose reports made by officers of the 1st Dragoons respecting Sharps' Carbines.

These reports fully sustain my recommendations in regard to said arms.
                        Respectfully, I am, sir, your obedient servant.
                                        W. A. THORNTON,
                                        BREVET MAJOR U. S. ARMY.
COL. H. K. CRAIG,
    UNITED STATES CORPS OF ORDNANCE.

Endorsement.

ORDNANCE OFFICE, April 13th, 1858.

The enclosed reports on Sharps' Carbines are respectfully submitted to the Secretary of War for his consideration.   H. K. CRAIG,
                                        COL. OF ORDNANCE.

FORT BUCHANAN, N. M., February 25th, 1858.

SIR:—I have the honor to acknowledge the receipt of your letter of November 18th, (delayed by being missent,) requesting a report upon Sharps' Carbines.

I have reported strongly in favor of the weapon at different times during the four years that a few have been in my company, and have no reason to change my views.

It is far superior to either rifle, musketoon, or carbine pistol, more particularly as a cavalry arm. There are minor parts of the weapon, sight, swivel-bar, &c., that are defective, but these would be soon improved after a little experience.

Not one of those in my company has become out of order in the breech-loading arrangement, (the peculiarity of the arm,) and the testing has been very severe. Mine have the Maynard primer, which is a failure.

Its lightness, rapidity of fire, range, accuracy, and facility of handling on horseback, make it highly suitable for mounted as well as dismounted service, and I urgently request that my company may be armed with them.

I do not know a cavalry officer who differs from these views.
                        Very respectfully, your obedient servant,
                                        R. S. EWELL,
                                        CAPT. 1ST DRAGOONS.
MAJ. W. A. THORNTON,
    ORDNANCE DEPARTMENT U. S. ARMY.

I fully concur in the above report, and every officer that has used the arm gives it the preference over all arms now in use, and I hope that they may be furnished the 1st Dragoons.   F. STEEN,
                                        MAJOR 1ST DRAGOONS, COMMANDING.

I fully concur in the foregoing report.   OWEN CHAPMAN,
                                        FIRST LIEUT. 1ST DRAGOONS.

FORT BUCHANAN, N. M., February 20th, 1858.

SIR :—Your note of November 19th, 1857, desiring information with regard to the serviceableness of Sharps' carbine for mounted troops, reached me yesterday.

As a breech-loading arm is the only one that can be used with any hope of success by a trooper in the saddle, it would be unnecessary to discuss the relative merits of this kind of fire-arm with those the loading of which requires the use of the rammer.

My experience has confirmed me in the belief that Sharps's carbine is far better adapted to mounted service than any other arm which has yet been introduced into the army; it combines the facility of loading when in the saddle with the range and accuracy of the rifle when on foot.

I have the honor to be, Major, very respectfully, your obedient servant,
D. B. HASTINGS,
FIRST LIEUTENANT 1ST DRAGOONS.

BVT. MAJ. W. A. THORNTON,
CAPT. ORDNANCE DEPARTMENT, Watervliet Arsenal, West Troy, N. Y

———

TEUSON, NEW MEXICO, Feb. 24th, 1858.

MAJOR :—I have the honor to report that the sixteen Sharps' Carbines which you sent to my company have been in constant use for four months, and that I find them greatly superior to any arm which has been furnished to any mounted troops under my command since I have been in the service. When a small detachment is sent on dangerous service it is invariably armed with them. The fire is rapid and accurate, and the ball is thrown a long distance. The objection that the paper remains in the chamber of the piece after the explosion of the cartridge, is easily obviated by extracting it with the little finger. I have known on two occasions forty rounds to be fired in rapid succession without inconvenience from the above cause. I have never known an accident to occur with them.   I am very respectfully, your obedient servant,
EDWARD H. FITZGERALD,
CAPT. 1ST DRAGOONS, AND BREVET MAJOR COMMANDING CO. B.

MAJ. W. A. THORNTON,
ORDNANCE CORPS, Watervliet Arsenal, N. Y.

———

FORT BUCHANAN, N. M., February 10, 1858.

MAJOR :—I have for several years past used myself, and have had in the company I have the honor now to command, Sharps' carbines, in constant use. I consider it the most superior small arm I have ever seen ; in my opinion, for dragoon service, there is no arm to compare with it for efficiency and convenience.

I would suggest from experience, as an improvement, that the sights, &c., be made finer, and that the angle between the stock and barrel produced be slightly increased.

I have had the honor, in my requisition for the next six months, to apply that this arm be furnished Brevet Maj. J. H. Carleton's company.

I have the honor to be, Major, very respectfully, your ob't servant,
A. B. CHAPMAN,
2D LIEUTENANT 1ST DRAGOONS, COMMANDING CO. K.

MAJ. W. A. THORNTON,
ORDNANCE CORPS, U. S. A., Watervliet Arsenal, N. Y.

———

FORT BUCHANAN, N. M., March 15th, 1858.

SIR :—I respectfully beg the honorable Secretary of War, through you, the chief of ordnance, that my company, (B, 1st Dragoons,) may be armed with Sharps' carbines, having, I believe, Major Thornton's improvements, and mounted with the saddle of the pattern of 1857, commonly called among us the McClellan saddle ; and that these arms and equipments, 85 of each, may be sent to the destination of the company in California. I am satisfied from trial and experience, that Sharps' carbine is the best weapon yet known in our country for a cavalry soldier. Its range and accuracy are greater than those of the musketoon. It is a stronger arm ; the soldier can make it last longer. The swivels and muzzles of the musketoon are constantly getting broken and battered.

The range of the Sharps is as great as that of the new carbine pistol—its accuracy of fire greater. The Sharps can be loaded at full speed ; the carbine pistol can not without great inconvenience. I am satisfied that the horseman needs no pistol if armed with Sharps' carbine and a light and sharp sabre.   *   *   *   *

One argument, I had almost omitted to mention, in favor of Sharps' carbine, is, that dragoon soldiers have more confidence in it than any other weapon I have ever seen put into their hands; and I have seen them use the musketoon, carbine pistol and Minie rifle. Give your soldiers but confidence in the effectiveness of their weapons, and they will give a better account of themselves than with those they can not trust.

Hoping that my request for the arming and mounting of my company, impelled by no other motive than the efficiency of the men I command, may meet with favor and attention, I am, sir, most respectfully, your obedient servant,

J. W. DAVIDSON,
CAPTAIN 1ST DRAGOONS, COMMANDING Co. B.

We, officers of the company, concur in the above.

OWEN CHAPMAN,
1ST LIEUTENANT 1ST DRAGOONS.

COL. H. K. CRAIG,
ORDNANCE DEPARTMENT.

B. F. DAVIS,
2D LIEUTENANT 1ST DRAGOONS.

ORDNANCE OFFICE, April 17th, 1858.

Respectfully referred to the Secretary of War, in connection with letters of similar purport referred from this office on the 13th instant.

H. K. CRAIG,
COLONEL OF ORDNANCE.

WAR DEPARTMENT, WASHINGTON, April 17th, 1858.

I certify that the foregoing letters from ——— Brevet Major W. A. Thornton, with the endorsement of Col. H. K. Craig, Chief of Ordnance; Captain R. S. Ewell, Major E. Steen, and Lieut. O. Chapman; Lièut. D. H. Hastings, Captain Edward H. Fitzgerald, and Lieut. A. B. Chapman, are true copies, and that the letter from ——— Captain J. W. Davidson, endorsed by Col. H. K. Craig, Chief of Ordnance, is a true extract; all from the originals on file in this department.

W. R. DRINKARD,
CHIEF CLERK.

FORT BUCHANAN, NEW MEXICO, March 27th, 1858.

MAJOR—I learn from Major Fitzgerald, of my Regiment, that you will send Sharps' Carbine to those companies of the Regiment who report favorably of the arm.

I had before learning this, made an application to the Secretary of War, through the Chief of Ordnance for Sharps' Carbine. I not only report favorably on Sharps' Carbine, but consider it with the improvements you have added to it, as the best weapon for a Cavalry soldier known to me.

You will find in my application to Col. Craig all the reasons which induce me to apply for Sharps', and I respectfully ask you to favor my application, and have 85 of these guns sent to the destination of my company.

The men have perfect confidence in this weapon, and this is half the battle.

It can be loaded at speed, and I have said to Col. Craig, that with a Sharps' Carbine and Sabre, that I do not want the pistol for my company. A wounded man on the ground can load and fire and use as effectually one of these Carbines as he could a revolver.

I am, Sir, very respectfully your obedient servant,
(Signed)   J. W. DAVIDSON,
CAPT. 1ST DRAGOONS COMMANDING COMPANY B.

True copy,

W. A. THORNTON,
BREVET MAJOR UNITED STATES ARMY.

EXTRACTS FROM LETTERS RECEIVED FROM THOSE WHO HAVE USED THE ARM.

MATAGORDA, TEXAS, April 3d, 1853.

MR. C. SHARPS :—I have had some experience with one of your rifles, and think it the best, most safe, and in fact it is the only gun now known for western hunting. I think if your guns were introduced here, you could scarcely fill the orders from this state. HENRY JONES.

BRUNSWICK, FLORIDA, October 4th, 1853.

I have had two hunts with my little shot gun, (21 inch barrel.) Yesterday I killed twenty-five quails. There were three gentlemen with me using the old fashioned double-barrel guns; I spent half my time waiting for them to load, and if I had pressed on could have killed all the birds. This arm will kill at a greater distance than any of their long guns. Every one is charmed with it.

D. C. HUBBARD.

LAS LUNAS, NEW MEXICO, March 18th, 1854.

I have had five of Sharps' carbines on hand six months, and am satisfied that they are superior to any firearm yet furnished the dragoons.

R. S. EWELL,
CAPTAIN 1ST DRAGOONS,

MAGOFFANSVILLE, TEXAS, June, 1853.

The ten Sharps' carbines purchased of you were all put to immediate use in arming my escort, and for range, accuracy, and rapidity of firing, they are far superior to any arm known. They have gone through what an ordnance officer would term a pretty severe field test, without the least injury.

In all of our shooting of bear, deer, wolves, &c., I have never known the ball to be found in the animal. Having been a frontier man for fourteen years, I had occasion to look after a bosom companion to stand by me in case of life or death; and hence I have given some little attention to the subject of fire arms, and think I can tolerably well appreciate their excellence; and in my search after such a comforter, I have found no arm that in all its attributes begins to compare with the Sharps' arm and for army, navy, caravan or sporting service, it is sure to take and hold the front rank.

CAPT. HENRY SKILLMAN,
U. S. MAIL CONTRACTOR.

From a letter written by Gov. Stevens, who led the Northern Pacific Railroad Exploring Expedition.

WASHINGTON, D. C., June 26th, 1854.

The Sharps' rifles issued for the service of the exploration under my charge, proved excellent and reliable arms. They can be used on horseback at full speed, and the limited number in our hands served to increase our numbers.

ISAAC D. STEVENS.

WASHINGTON, January, 1855.

In answer to your inquiries, I take great pleasure in bearing testimony to the great value and use of Sharps' rifles. Upon two expeditions across the continent to California, I have had the ten rifles in active use the whole time in the field. With ten men armed with these rifles we felt equal to thirty. Its simplicity enabled the men to understand it at a glance, and they loaded and fired it with great accuracy and rapidity, killing game at four hundred and fifty yards. It inspired the men with great confidence in their strength and power to defend themselves against superior numbers. With ten men, a negro and a Mexican, I kept at bay one hundred and forty Apache warriors, all fully armed, just on the eve of an attack on Gov. Gardner's ranch in Sonora. I look upon it as far the best rifle and the only proper one for mounted men that I have ever seen. ANDREW B. GRAY.

From a letter from Col. Fremont.

WASHINGTON CITY, June 19th, 1854.

In my journey last winter to California I took with me two of Sharps' rifles, one designed for use on horseback, and one for my own use, of the usual western rifle length and weight. I found it the most convenient gun I ever used.

J. C. FREMONT.

WASHINGTON, January, 1855.

I have used the Sharps' rifle for some time as a defense of the U. S. mail from Inde pendence to Santa Fe. I believe it the best arm for use on the plains now in existence, carrying with great precision and force from four to six hundred yards. I have frequently killed deer, antelope and buffalo at a distance of over four hundred yards.

JACOB HALL.

SAN ANTONIO, TEXAS, February 10th, 1855.

It affords me great pleasure to bear testimony from actual experience to the merits of Sharps' rifle. I have used it for two years, a part of the time over my mail route, and it has proved a saviour to myself and my men, when any other arm would have failed me. As for killing bear, deer, &c., I will pit Sharps' rifle against all other arms known.

G. H. GIDDINGS,
MAIL CONTRACTOR FROM SAN ANTONIO TO SANTA FE.

MADISON, WISCONSIN, March 15th, 1856.

J. C. PALMER, ESQ.—DEAR SIR: Yours of February was duly received. I am obliged for the instructions, &c. I had become entirely satisfied with the rifle I have. A match at shooting came off here this week at 200 yards. I got two shots at the target; first ball one inch under the center; second ball half an inch, and the target was taken down. I don't believe a better or truer rifle can be made. Can shoot seven balls out of ten 200 yards into a two inch ring, if the wind does not blow; can tell where the ball strikes without going to see. Did shoot two gang of deer, three in the first and five in the second, and got all but one without moving ten feet. This is sufficient for me. I can beat any marksman here his own distance. The rifle works fine, and is completely made in every respect; never saw better work or better shooting than I have made. I shall make the feathers fly from the turkeys forty rods, but should like to shoot eighty rods against forty, which I can do with a glass.

Yours respectfully,
H. A. TIFFANY.

FORT CAPRON, FLORIDA, January 1st, 1856.

MR. J. C. PALMER, Sharps' Rifle Manufacturing Company, Hartford, Conn.

SIR:—I desire to volunteer my opinion as to the superiority of Sharps' rifle and Sharps' rifle carbine over all other arms for sporting and military purposes.

For rapidity of loading and firing, penetration of the ball and extent of range, it is much preferable to any rifle I have ever seen. The objection sometimes alleged, and the only one I ever heard of, that the cartridge wrapper may remain in the barrel, may be remedied by the use of strong yellow "envelope paper," but in any case the use of the finger will remove the remnant in an instant. Thirty or forty rounds may be fired before this becomes necessary.

In all military operations where a bayonet is not required, as in scouting, skirmishing, and particularly for mounted service, it is without an equal.

I have used Sharps' and the Maynard primer—I regard the former as decidedly the best.   I am, very respectfully,

EDWARD C. BOYNTON,
BREVET CAPTAIN U. S. ARMY

A letter from General Hornsby.

WASHINGTON, April 12, 1858.

SHARPS' RIFLE MANUFACTURING COMPANY—GENTLEMEN:—In answer to your inquiry as to my experience with Sharps' Rifles, I take pleasure in saying, that for three years past I have been very familiar with your Rifles and others, Colt's among the number, in Nicaragua and elsewhere, and I have no hesitation in saying, that for safety, range, accuracy and efficiency, your arm proved itself vastly superior to all others. A prejudice obtains against Colt's Rifle from frequent accidental discharges, its liability to get out of order, and from its being more difficult to load in an engagement than a muzzle loading arm, and furthermore the soldiers used them in fear. On the contrary, your arm inspired confidence, and the soldier took the risk of accident from a single charge—he could not, when loaded, insert the second, and the arrangement is such as to make the bore of the barrel open to instant inspection, cleaning, loading under the greatest speed on horseback, in ambush, or in the open field. Ten rounds at aim are easily fired in one minute with your arm ; three seconds are sufficient to clean it after firing 100 rounds, and in my opinion, it has no equal. In conclusion, not to go into further particulars, I can say your arm has the requisite strength in all its parts, is not liable to get out of order, and is well adapted to use.

Your obedient servant,
C. C. HORNSBY.

WASHINGTON, D. C., May 21st, 1858.

GENTLEMEN :—I have used Sharps' Rifle for about four years, as a defense of the United States Mail, from Independence, Mo., to Santa Fe, N. M., and the longer I use it, the more firm are my convictions, expressed to you in January, 1855, " that it is the best arm for use on the plains now in existence." The rapidity with which it can be fired—ten times a minute in the hands of one skilled in its use—its precision, force and extent of range, its freeness from liability of getting out of order, are all superior to any other arm to which my attention has been called. Nor are the primers uncertain, as I have heard it sometimes asserted. I have frequently discharged a magazine of fifty primers without missing fire more than once or twice. I still continue to use them on the plains, and expect to continue their use as long as I am contractor for the mail on the plains.

Yours very respectfully, &c.,
JACOB HALL,
U. S. MAIL CONTRACTOR FROM INDEPENDENCE, MO., TO SANTA FE, N. M.

A letter from Col. E. E. Cross.

HACIENDA DE SANTA RITA, ARIZONA, January 30, 1859.

PRESIDENT OF SHARPS' RIFLE COMPANY—DEAR SIR,—After trying all the breech loading arms of the day, I fall back upon your valuable arm. It is the greatest weapon of the age. Three hundred of them would sell in this territory at from $75 to $85 each. The rifle sent me by your concern, last August, I used all the way across the Plains to Tubac, where it was stolen. I want another. Please get me up a sporting rifle, 24 inch barrel, " half-ounce" ball, fine sight and good finish, and send to me, via overland mail, care Postmaster at Teuson. I would be glad if you would attend to this at once.

Yours truly,
E. E. CROSS.

REPORT

OF

THE SECRETARY OF WAR,

IN ANSWER TO

A resolution of the Senate calling for information in relation to Sharps' rifle carbine.

MARCH 9, 1859.—Ordered to lie on the table. Motion to print referred to the Committee on Printing. Report in favor of printing submitted, considered, and agreed to.

WAR DEPARTMENT, March 7, 1859.

SIR,—In response to the inquiries contained in a resolution of the Senate, of the 5th instant, respecting Sharps' Rifle Carbine. I have the honor herewith to transmit a report of the Colonel of Ordnance giving the information desired.

Very respectfully, your obedient servant,

JOHN B. FLOYD,
SECRETARY OF WAR.

HON. J. C. BRECKINRIDGE,
PRESIDENT OF THE SENATE.

ORDNANCE OFFICE, WASHINGTON, March 7, 1859.

SIR,—In answer to the resolution of the Senate, dated 5th instant, I have the honor to state : Sharps' Carbine has been issued for arming a portion of the mounted troops of the United States army, and has been in use by those troops for about five years. The reports from officers who have had this arm in use, by troops under their command, are of different character. The majority report favorably as to its efficiency and serviceableness in the field ; while some officers report unfavorably in regard to these points.

The unfilled requisitions for these arms, which are now on file, are as follows, viz : A letter from General Harney, dated September 14, 1858, asking that Sharps' carbines may be sent for the troops serving in Oregon to such an extent as to make up, with those on hand there, the number of 4,000 ; a requisition from Captain Whiteley, commanding the arsenal at San Antonio, dated February 7, 1859, for 500 of these arms for the use of the troops in the military department of Texas, none of which had been supplied ; a requisition from Colonel Bonneville, commanding the military department of New Mexico, dated January 11, 1859, for 200 of these arms, of which 150 have been ordered to be supplied, leaving 50 still due on that requisition ; and a requisition from Captain E. A. Carr, of the 1st Regiment of Cavalry, dated January 11, 1859, for 85 of these arms for the use of his company, none of which have been supplied.

The reasons for the non-fulfillment of these requisitions are as follows : As regards General Harney's requisition, in my letter to you of the 16th September, 1858, transmitting the General's request, it was stated, "this department has not a sufficient store of the arms asked for him to meet his requisition, nor has it the means of making the purchase necessary to enable it to do so." Colonel Bonneville's requisition was reduced from 200 to 150, because there were only the latter number remaining in the arsenals unissued to the troops ; and the requisitions of Captain Whiteley and Captain Carr were not filled in whole or in part, because the supply of these arms at the arsenals had been exhausted by previous issues to the troops.

The resolution of the Senate is returned herewith.

Very respectfully your obedient servant,

H. K. CRAIG,
COLONEL OF ORDNANCE.

HON. J. B. FLOYD,
SECRETARY OF WAR.

BRIDGEPORT, CONN., AUGUST 10th, 1880.

Owing to the pressing demand for Rifles with outside lock and hammer, the Company have finished and can now deliver a limited number of

SHARPS RIFLES, SPECIAL MODEL, 1874,

with case-hardened Systems, Knife Blade Front Sights, polished stocks, *and having barrels fully up to our own high standard of excellence.*

These Arms all being completed, orders for this model varying from the descriptions given below, cannot be filled.

The 40 calibre. 2¼ inch bottle neck chamber, 70 grains, and 40 calibre 2¼ inch straight chamber, 65 grains, may be rechambered to take the 2⅝ inch bottle neck, 90 grain shell. Also the 45 calibre, 2 1-10 inch chamber, 70 grains, may be rechambered to take the 2⅞ inch, 90 to 110 grain shell. To order only. Price of rechambering, $1.

The capacity of the 45 calibre, 2⅞ inch shell, is from 90 to 110 grains of powder, the quantity being dependent on the grade of powder used and the care exercised in slowly filling it.

Style of Rifle.	Cal.	Style of Barrel.	L'gth of Bbl.	Chamber.	Trigger.	Weight.	Price.
Saddle Rifles,	.40	H'lf Oct'g'n	26 in.	2 1-4 N'ked, 70 grs.	D'ble.	8 to 9 lbs.	$25 00
" "	.40	Octagon	26 in.	2 1-4 N'ked, 70 grs.	D'ble.	8 to 9 lbs.	25 00
" "	.45	H'lf Oct'g'n	26 in.	2 1-10 Stght, 70 grs.	S'gle.	8 to 9 lbs.	22 00
Business "	.45	Round	28 in.	2 1-10 Stght, 70 grs.	D'ble.	10½ lbs.	26 00
Sporting "	.45	Octagon	28 in.	2 1-10 Stght, 70 grs.	S'gle.	8 to 9 lbs.	23 00
" "	.45	Octagon	28 in.	2 1-10 Stght, 70 grs.	D'ble.	8 to 9 lbs.	26 00
" "	.45	Hl'f Oct'g'n	30 in.	2 1-10 Stght, 70 grs.	D'ble.	ab't 10 lbs.	26 00
" "	.45	Octagon	30 in.	2 1-10 Stght, 70 grs.	D'ble.	10½to11½	28 00
" "	.45	Octagon	30 in.	2 7-8 Stght, 90to110	D'ble.	11to12 lbs.	28 50
" "	.45	Octagon	30 in.	2 7-8 Stght, 90to110	D'ble.	14to16 lbs.	33 50
" "	.40	Octagon	30 in.	2 1-2 Stght, 65 grs.	D'ble.	10½to11½	28 00

Globe and Peep Sights, (with Wind Guage in Peep Sight,) as shown on page 16 and 17 of this Catalogue, will be furnished complete with these arms when ordered, at $3 list, per set.

Military Wind Guage Slides, interchangeable with regular slide on Model 1878,

Military Sight, can now be furnished. List Price, - - - -	$1 00
Buck Horn Rear Sights, complete. - - - - - - -	2 00
Spirit Level Glasses, - - - - - - - -	25
Bullet Swages, - - - - - - - - -	6 00

Owing to the increased cost of labor and material, the list prices of 1878 Model Rifles were, on May 1st, 1880, advanced as follows:

Sporting Rifles, Model 1878, to - - - - - - -	$30 00
Business " " " " - - - - - -	28 00
Hunters' " " " " - - - - - -	25 00

SHARPS RIFLE COMPANY.

B. KITTREDGE & CO.

SHARPS TRIUMPH, (2 1-2.)

32 CARTRIDGE.

Cut is exact size of Pistol.

The Sharps Pistol was invented by Christian Sharps After several hundred thousand .22 and .30 calibre pistols were made and sold these pistols were all made with brass or gun metal frames), the inventor conceived the idea of doing something better, and after several years, and after a large expenditure of money and labor, produced a pistol more compact, yet of much larger calibre. To do this, he abandoned the brass frame, making the pistol wrought throughout and of the very best material and workmanship. The cut represents the pistol, and is the exact size. It occupies less room in the pocket than any so large calibre pistol ever made. Shortly after this new pistol came out, Mr. Sharps died; the manufacture ceased, and the factory, etc., were sold. B Kittredge & Co. bought the entire product of this pistol. We call it SHARPS TRIUMPH. We claim for it compactness, strong shooting, and simplicity It has all the advantages of the cylinder pistols, and shoots with greater penetration, there being no power lost by the escape, as in a cylinder pistol, between the barrel and cylinder. It is very durable, there being but few parts, strong, and thoroughly well made We have never seen a frame broken or barrel burst out of over 15,000 sold by us. We have a few hundred left which we propose to sell at $5.50 for wood handle and plated frame; 30 cents extra if full plate; $1.50 extra for ivory handle. And we propose, further, to deliver the pistol free if within 500 miles; 25 cents extra over 500 in the United States. Send us post-office order and the pistol will come to you without charge.

CARTRIDGES.—In purchasing cartridges for Colt's New Line, *insist* upon having 22, .30, .38, and 4 *long* These sizes *short* are intended for pistols with cast-iron frames. All will fit in Colt's New Line, but the long are required for best penetration We may here mention that there is a way in boring cast-iron pistols, which is to make the barrel the size, or nearly the size, of the cylinder. This takes off the strain so that cast-iron may stand it; *but it destroys the penetration.*

NOTICE.—Reductions in Price Lists of other Pistols

	Price	Ivory Extra.	Pear Extra.		Price.	Ivory Extra.	Pearl Extra.
.22 O M Colt	$3.75	$0.75	$2.75	.44 Cartridge (Army)	$12.00	$3.00	$1.00
.22 Little Colt	5.00	.75	1.75	.38 Navy	5.00		
.30 Pony Colt	6.75	.75	1.75	.41 House	6.50		.40
.32 Ladies' Colt	6.75	.75	1.75	.38 D A. Lightning	17.50	2.75	.60
.38 Pet Colt	8.00	1.00	2.50	.41 D. A Thunderer	17.00	2.75	.60
.41 Big Colt	8.50	1.00	2.50	.36 S. & W	12.00	2.75	.60
.45 Peacemaker (Army)	6.50	3.00		.46 S. & W. Army	15.00	3.50	1.00
.44 Army Old Line	7.50	3.00					

Also, a full line of low-priced pistols—a multitude of names and makers. We deliver at above prices on receipt of price at our cost for delivery, if within 500 miles.

Breech-Loading and Self-Priming Rifle, Carbine and Shot Gun,

MANUFACTURED ONLY BY THE

SHARPS' RIFLE MANUFACTURING COMPANY,

AT HARTFORD, CONNECTICUT.

SHARPS' PATENT

SHARPS'

PATENT BREECH-LOADING AND SELF-PRIMING

Rifle, Carbine and Shot-Gun.

———◆•◆•◆———

THESE Arms have now attained the highest perfection in every respect; the primes are carefully prepared, are water proof and *sure fire*—the sights are of a new and most approved pattern, the gas check shuts off every particle of escape, and the manufacturers challenge the world to produce an Arm of superior material, strength, accuracy, force, safety or rapidity and certainty of fire. They are self-priming, with either Sharps' or 'Maynard's' primer, and adapted likewise to the use of the Army percussion cap. The barrel is of Cast Steel, and its chamber, or ball seat, is counter-bored, slightly conical, the exact shape and diameter of the ball, so that the ball, when properly forced to its seat, has its axis exactly coincident with that of the bore; the rear of the bore contains an adjustable bouching, and the space between its forward end and the base of the ball receives the dirt that otherwise might partially obstruct the ball in finding its seat, and likewise admits the clamp and rod, with which the bouching is driven back in adjusting it. The concavity in the face of the slide, after a number of fires, should be cleaned; as in the chamber of every kind of fire-arm, after repeated discharges, a collection of Sulphate of Potassa is found in hard substance.

To CLEAN THE ARM, relieve the lever key from pressure, by throwing down the lever guard, and then take out the key, which is replaced, with the guard in the same position. Remove the slide and dissolve the hard substance with water if any has collected in its cavity, taking care not to use any metalic tool in the operation, by which the slide, or gas-ring, might be injured. The bore is easily washed, or cleansed with a wet brush, after which, wipe it quite dry, and oil it, and the slide, with sperm oil, tallow or other pure oil, free from salt and acids.

To CHARGE THE LOCK WITH "SHARPS' PRIMES," cock the Arm, shove back the magazine cover on the top surface of the lock-plate, by pressing the left thumb against the screw head beneath the cup of the hammer. Withdraw the tack nail from the charging tube, insert the primer's end of this tube in the magazine with the left hand, the slot in the tube in line with the slot in the face of the lock-plate, and press it down as far as the spiral spring will admit, then with the right hand thrust the tack nail through the slots in the tube and lock-plate above the primes, withdraw the tube, bring the lock to half-cock and withdraw the tack nail. The priming magazine charged, the cover must not be moved back, lest the primes escape. Nor should the hammer be worked, between half and full cock, for the same reason.

Sharps' Arms made for using "Maynard's primer," are similar in their arrangement for its use, to other Army Guns adapted to it.

IN LOADING SHARPS' GUNS, clasp the arm in front of the lock with the left hand, throw down the lever guard with the right, and insert the cartridge with the same, pressing it forcibly into its seat in the bore; then draw the lever smartly to its position, thus cutting of the end of the cartridge. Incline the arm to the right or left to throw off the superfluous powder, from the groove on the top of the slide. Let the hammer remain down while loading, and never open the breech whilst the arm is loaded, without dropping the muzzle, so as to bring the barrel to a vertical position.

Percussion Caps are used as with other guns. After a number of discharges, the ball is more readily entered into its seat, by working the cartridge back and forward a few times, before pressing it home.

THE PROPER CHARGE for Army Rifles and Carbines is 55 to 60 grains of powder of 300 yards eprouvette range; and cartridges are used for convenience and celerity in firing. In using loose ammunition the barrel must be held vertically, with the muzzle down, the ball is inserted and forced to its seat with a short rod, and the powder charge is poured upon it, and the slide closed. In all firings without patches, the balls must be coated with tallow, to prevent the bore from *leading*.

Cartridges made of the exact length of the chamber, having their ends closed with thin muslin or gauze, are preferred by some. Such cartridges are not cut off; the fire of the primes penetrating the cartridge through its rear end.

The Receiver is of the best wrought iron, case hardened. *After the barrel has been screwed into the Receiver and the slide fitted, it should not be unscrewed*, except in case of necessity, and by a competent mechanic. *The Slide*, which closes the rear end of the barrel, is cast steel, hardened. In its face a steel ring is inserted, around the circumference of a concavity, in the centre of which the vent enters. The ring is called a "gas check," the action of the charge, when fired, against its inner surface, forcing it out, an imperceptible distance, against the rear end of the bouching, so as to close the joint and prevent the escape of any portion of the force of the fired charge.

IN TAKING OFF THE LOCK, give four turns out, to the side

screws; then strike their heads with the screw-driver, which will start the lock from its bed. The side screws will then be taken out, and the lock can be removed.

To REPLACE THE LOCK, press it firmly into its bed before entering the screws, and then turn them up close.

Numerous reports from the Ordnance, and other Army Boards, and letters and certificates on file in the Ordnance Office at Washington, attest the superior quality and efficiency of Sharps' Rifles and Carbines, which have withstood every test, and the most satisfactory of all, three or four years service in the field, in the hands of U. S. Troops; and on board our ships of War. They have also been supplied, in large numbers, to the British Government, and are highly esteemed in the English service.

Sporting Rifles have been sold in such great numbers that their merits are fully appreciated. The recent improvements having removed the only defect, the escape of gas at the joint, these arms are now recommended, as being as nearly perfect as practicable.   SAMUEL H. GREEN, *Sec'y.*

HARTFORD, January 1, 1859.

SHARPS' PATENT

IMPROVED

BREECH-LOADING & SELF-PRIMING

Rifle, Carbine, and Shot Gun,

MANUFACTURED ONLY BY THE

SHARPS' RIFLE MANUFACTURING CO.,

AT

HARTFORD, CONNECTICUT,

WITH

MANUAL, INSTRUCTIONS, RECOMMENDATIONS

AND COMPONENT PARTS.

— ·· —

HARTFORD:
PRESS OF CASE, LOCKWOOD AND COMPANY.
MAY 1, 1864.

SHARPS' PATENT

IMPROVED BREECH-LOADING AND SELF-PRIMING

RIFLE, CARBINE AND SHOT-GUN.

———•◆•———

THESE arms have now attained the highest perfection in every respect. The proprietors have adopted all the improvements that fourteen years of experience could suggest. The primes are carefully prepared, are water proof and *sure fire*—the arms and their parts are of new and most approved patterns, the gas-check shuts off every particle of escape, and the manufacturers challenge the world to produce an arm of superior material, strength, accuracy, force, safety or rapidity and certainty of fire. They are self-priming, with SHARPS' PRIMER, and adapted likewise to the use of the army percussion cap. The barrel is of cast steel, and its chamber or ball-seat, is counter-bored, slightly conical, the precise shape and diameter of the bearings of the ball, so that the ball, when properly forced to its seat, has its axis exactly coincident with that of the bore; the rear of the bore contains an adjustable bouching, and the space between its forward end and the base of the ball admits the clamp and rod, with which the bouching is driven back in adjusting it.

The arm when cleaned and properly oiled should, before loading, have a primer or cap snapped off to remove the oil.

The Receiver is of the best wrought iron, case hardened. *After the barrel has been screwed into the Receiver and the slide fitted, it should not be unscrewed*, except in case of necessity, and by a competent mechanic. *The Slide,* which closes the rear end of the barrel, is cast steel, hardened. In its face a steel ring attached to a face-plate is inserted, around the circumference of a concavity, in the centre of which the vent enters. The ring and plate is called a "gas-check," the action of the charge, when fired, against its inner surface, forcing it out, an imperceptible distance, against the rear end of the bouching, so as to close the joint and prevent the escape of any portion of the force of the fired charge.

IN TAKING OFF THE LOCK, give four turns out, to the side screws; then strike their heads with the screw-driver, which will start the lock from its bed. The side screws will then be taken out, and the lock can be removed.

TO RE-PLACE THE LOCK, press it firmly into its bed before entering the screws, and then turn them up close.

Numerous reports from the Ordnance, and other army Boards, and letters and certificates on file in the Ordnance Office at Washington, attest the superior quality and efficiency of Sharps' rifles and carbines, which have withstood every test, and the most satisfactory of all, twelve years service in the field in the hands of United States troops, and on board our ships of war. They have also been supplied in large numbers to the British, Spanish, Mexican, Peruvian, Chilian, Venezuelian and Japanese governments, and are highly esteemed in the service. More than this, it is the *only breech-loading arm* of any account in which *loose powder and ball* can be practically used with effect or safety; others requiring a very expensive and peculiar kind of fixed ammunition which can not be prepared in the field and is of no service except it be used in the particular style of arm for which it was prepared.

The great superiority of our arm is fully established in the experience of this country in its present war.

It is the arm demanded by and furnished to the *sharp-shooters*, after fully testing the various other styles presented, not without injury to themselves in some cases, and it is the first choice of the masses of both infantry and cavalry as a service arm.

Sporting rifles have been sold in such great numbers that their merits are fully appreciated. The recent improvements having removed the only defect, the escape of gas at the joint, these arms are now recommended as being the most perfect arm of the times.

In point of material, workmanship, and accuracy or rapidity of fire, as compared with any other muzzle-loading, breech-loading, or revolving fire-arm that can be produced, we say try it, and if the trial does not attest its superiority, we shall be disappointed.

At the siege of Arequipa, Peru, in March, 1858, over 600 of Vivanco's men were shot down at the barricades by Castilla's attacking forces, armed with *Sharp's rifles*, sustaining only a trifling loss.

In April, 1858, Colonel Suasue, at the head of 1,000 men of Vidauri's force, armed with *Sharps' carbines*, attacked Governor Manero in command of 3,000 men of the government forces at San Louis, in Mexico, and achieved a most signal victory, killing upwards of 600 men, taking the city and making prisoners of Governor Manero and three of his colonels, with a slight loss.

About the 1st of September, 1858, Colonel Wright's command, principally armed with Sharps' carbines, were engaged with the party of Indians that had previously defeated Colonel Steptoe's forces, when armed with the old muskets and carbines. The engagement resulted in a most disastrous route and defeat of the Indians, with a loss of fifty warriors killed and wounded, while of Colonel Wright's force not a man was harmed.

We append some testimonials of the efficiency of our arms hitherto manufactured, as a guarantee of their utility.

SAMUEL H. GREEN, *Secretary.*

J. C. PALMER, *President.*

HARTFORD, May 1, 1864.

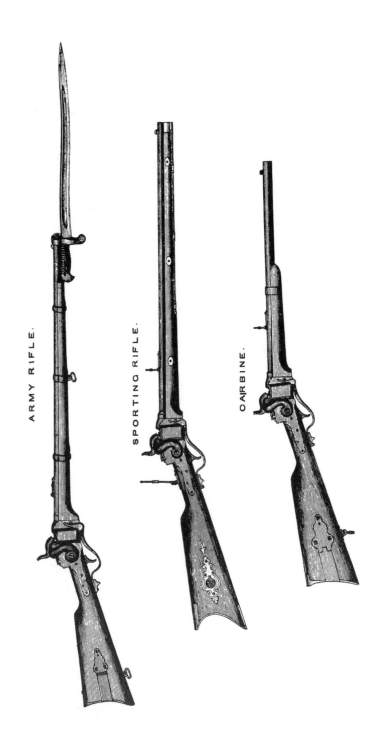

ARMY RIFLE.

SPORTING RIFLE.

CARBINE.

MANUAL FOR SHARPS' RIFLE.

1. Present Arms.
2. Shoulder Arms.
3. Order Arms.
4. Ground Arms.
5. Raise Arms.
6. Shoulder Arms.
7. Support Arms.
8. Shoulder Arms.
9. *Fix Bayonet.*
10. *Shoulder Arms.*
11. *Charge Bayonet.*
12. *Shoulder Arms.*
13. Trail Arms.
14. Shoulder Arms.
15. *Unfix Bayonet.*
16. *Shoulder Arms.*
17. Secure Arms.
18. Shoulder Arms.

The above is adapted to the rifle with bayonet; if no bayonet is attached, Nos. 9, 10, 11, 12, 15 and 16 are omitted.

LOADING.

The piece being at the shoulder, the order is given,

Prepare to Load.

Half face to the right, the same as the first motion of charge bayonet, drop the piece into the left hand, seizing it at base of the Tip, resting the Butt firmly against the hip; with the right hand throw down the Lever opening the Breech, await the order—

Load.

With the right hand take the Cartridge from the cartridge box, place it in the Breech and press it home smartly with the thumb, bring the Lever back to its place and the Piece to the shoulder, dropping the left hand to the side, and at the same time bring the right foot back on a line with the left, await the orders—

Ready! Aim!! FIRE!!!

When it is desired to continue the firing, or to load directly after the firing, the order of "*Prepare to Load*," will be omitted, and the order of "*Load*" given when the piece is at an aim.

Load, drop the piece to the same position, and proceed as before.

To fix and unfix the Sabre Bayonet.

Fix—by seizing the Rifle firmly around the top band with the left hand; with the right draw the sabre and carefully enter the top end of the spline in the lower end of the matrix in the handle of the Sabre, and press downward until the catch has closed.

Unfix—Clasp the muzzle of the Rifle and Sabre-hilt with the left hand, so as to bring the ball of the middle finger on the head of the catch bolt, holding the hilt firmly with the thumb and forefinger; with the right hand clasp the arm around the top band, bringing the thumb slightly crooked under the sabre head, compress the catch-bolt and straighten the thumb vigorously at the same instant; this will detach the Sabre, and taking the hilt with the right hand return to the scabbard.

Observe these rules and you will not drop the Sabre.

The angular bayonet designed and manufactured by us is the most symmetrical, strong and perfect thing of its kind yet produced, and is adjusted in the same manner as the ordinary bayonet.

To clean the Arm,

Relieve the lever key from pressure by throwing down the lever guard, and then take out the key, which is replaced with the guard in the same position. Remove the slide, and dissolve the hard substance with water if any has collected in its cavity, taking care not to use any metallic tool in the operation, by which the slide or gas ring might be injured. The bore is easily washed, or cleaned with a wet brush, after which wipe it dry and oil it and the slide with sperm oil, tallow, or other pure oil free from salt and acids.

To charge the lock with "Sharps' Primers."

Cock the arm, shove back the magazine cover on the top surface of the lock plate, by pressing the left thumb against the screw head beneath the cup of the hammer. Insert the primer end of the charging tube in the magazine with the left hand, the slot in the tube facing rearward towards the breech, press it down as far as the spiral spring will admit, and with the right hand shove forward the primer holder by means of a spur which projects on the inner surface of the lock plate and withdraw the tube.

It is thus primed with great facility, and to let the primers on or shut them off at any time when the hammer is down, requires but an instant, and is effected by throwing the primer holder backward or forward, consequently the primers or caps can either be used at pleasure. When the arm is not loaded, do not snap off the primers for the fun of the thing, for by so doing the fire communication is being filled with particles of copper in which the fulminating powder is enveloped and is ultimately closed, but in firing the arm the scale of copper from the primer is uniformly thrown out of the fire communication by the escape of gas at the vent of the cone.

Let the hammer remain down while loading.

The proper Charge

For Army Rifles and Carbines is 55 to 60 grains of powder of 300 yards eprouvette range; and cartridges are used for convenience and celerity in firing. In using loose ammunition the barrel must be held vertically, with the muzzle down, the ball is inserted and forced to its seat with a short rod, and the powder charge is poured upon it and the slide closed. In all firings without patches, the balls must be coated with tallow to prevent the bore from *leading*.

DIRECTIONS FOR MAKING BALL CARTRIDGES.

Cartridge paper or linen cloth, cut in strips of one and three-eighth inches for the Army size ball, and two inches for the 60 and 90 ball, and of length sufficient to wind twice around the larger end of the cartridge stick and form a cylinder, securing the end with gluten or paste, withdraw the stick, place a piece of bank-note paper or gauze three-fourths of an inch square on the reverse end of the stick, form it over the end, apply the gluten or paste to the part which overlies the circumference of the stick, and insert in the cylinder, forcing it to the rear end and withdraw the stick. When the cylinder is dry, charge with sixty grains of powder and insert the rear end of the ball to the ring thereon, moistened with the adhesive preparation, and choke the cloth or paper into the ring of the ball.

Before casting balls smoke the mold and heat it; you will then obtain a more perfect ball than can be swedged or pressed.

———

DIRECTIONS FOR MAKING SHOT CARTRIDGES AND LOADING.

The Shot Gun can be used with loose ammunition, loading at th breech, with one ounce of shot and about sixty grains of powder; and although the powder does not fill the cavity at the breech, no danger need be apprehended. The use of Shot Cartridges has great advantages over any other method, and they are made as follows:

Place the conical part of the Cartridge Stick on the paper, as in diagram No. 1, wind the paper and twist and firmly compress the part of it projecting over the end of the stick; withdraw the stick and charge with one ounce of shot, covering with a wad suited to the bore of the barrel.

Place the straight end of the stick on the paper or linen cloth if preferred, as in diagram No. 2, and wind and secure the end of the paper or cloth with gluten or paste; withdraw the stick, and having stopped the rear end as in case of ball cartridges, charge with about fifty grains of powder, paste or tie the two parts together.

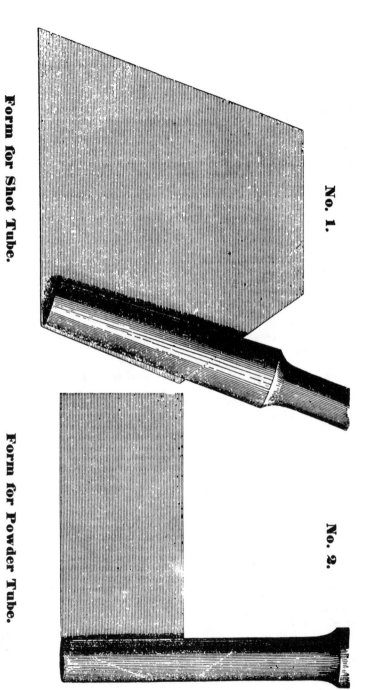

No. 1.

Form for Shot Tube.

No. 2.

Form for Powder Tube.

Component Parts of Rifle and Carbine, with Single or Double Trigger.

Barrel, (Rifle,)
" (Carbine,)
" Stud,
" Bouching,
Front Sight Stud,
" " Pin,
" " Silver,
Rear Sight Base Spring,
" " " " Screw,
" " " Pin,
" " Elevator,
" " Chair,
" " Slide,
" " " Screw.
Receiver,
Slide,
" Screw,
" Gas Plate,
Cone,
Slide Vent Tube,
" " " Screw,
Toggle,
" Screw,
Lever,
" Spring,
" " Screw,
" Key,
" " Stop Pin,
" " " Spring,
" " " " Screw,
" Catch,
" " Screw,
" " Spring,
" " " Screw,
" " " Pin,
Guard Strap, (Double Trigger,)
" " (Single Trigger,)
" " Screw Front,
" " " Rear,
Trigger, (Single)
" " Screw,
" (Double) Rear,
" " " Spring,
" " " " Screw,
" " " Pin,
" " Front,
" " " Spring,
" " " " Screw,
" " " Pin,
Lock Plate,
Hammer,
Tumbler,
" Fly,
" Screw,
" Stirrup,
" " Screw,
Main Spring,
" " Screw,
Sere,

Sere Screw,
Bridle,
" Screw,
Primer Spring,
" " Screw,
" Follower,
" " Pin,
" Driver,
" Slide,
" Shut Off
" " Screw,
" Covers,
" " Screw,
" " Pin,
Front Side Screw,
Rear " "
Front Tang "
Rear "
Stock Butt,
" " Escutcheon,
Butt Plate,
" " Screws,
Patch Box Head,
" " " Screws,
" " Lid,
" " Pin,
" " Spring,
" " " Screw,
" " Hook,
" " " Pins,
Stock Tip, (Carbine,)
" " (Rifle,)
" " Screw,
" " Escutcheon,
Nose Cap,
" " Screw,
Band, (Upper,)
" (Middle,)
" (Lower,)
" Carbine,
" Swivel,
" " Screw,
" Spring,
Swivel,
" Screw,
" Base,
" " Screws,
" Bar,
" " Screw,
" Ring,
Ball Mould,
Cone Wrench and Screw Driver,
Brush (Double,)
" (Single,)
Rod,
Cartridge Stick,
Thong, (Double,)
" (Single,)
Bouching Clamp and Rod.

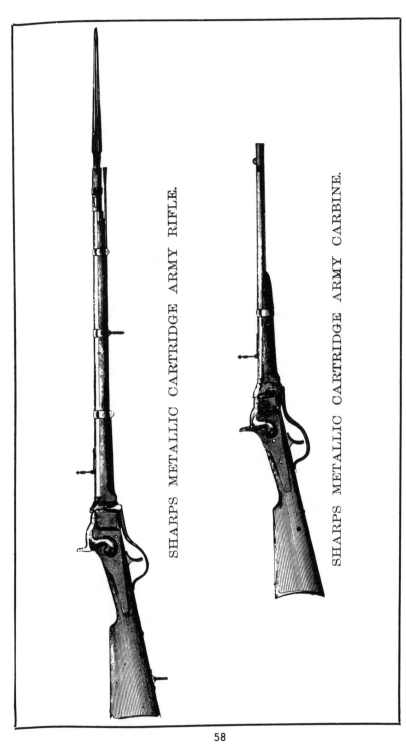

SHARPS METALLIC CARTRIDGE ARMY RIFLE.

SHARPS METALLIC CARTRIDGE ARMY CARBINE.

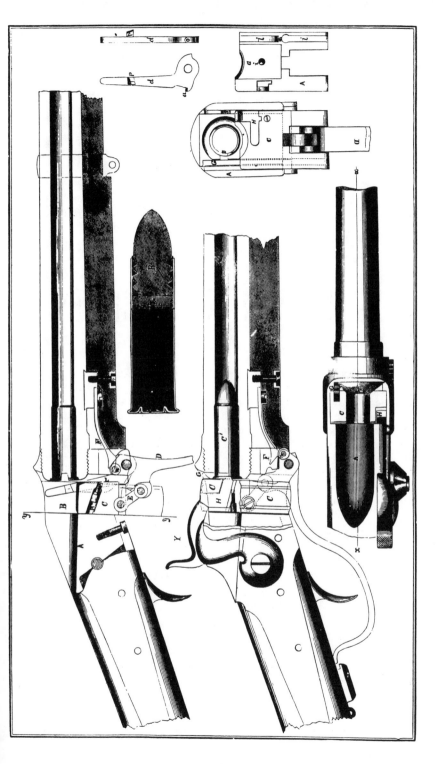

SHARPS PATENT

IMPROVED BREECH-LOADING

METALLIC CARTRIDGE

MILITARY RIFLES & CARBINES.

These arms have been largely in use for twenty-five years, and have been constantly growing in the favor of Military men. As War weapons their reputation among the officers and soldiers who served during the war for the Union, is far in advance of that of any other arm furnished by the Government.

A distinguished officer wrote : " *The men were so confident of the superiority of Sharps' Rifles, that they would at any time throw away their other weapons in action, to secure one dropped by a disabled comrade* "

As Military weapons, among their advantages, are :

FIRST.—Durability and simplicity when placed in the hands of ordinary soldiers.

SECOND.—The ease with which their several parts can be kept clean and in working order.

THIRD.—Their accuracy, both at short and long ranges.

FOURTH.—Their perfect safety, no accident ever having been known to result from any imperfection or fault of the weapons.

FIFTH.—The rapidity and uniformity of their fire. Fifteen rounds, at aim, are easily fired, in one minute ; and ten seconds is ample time for cleaning, after firing one hundred rounds.

By their arrangement, the bore of the barrel is open to instant inspection, and rapid loading is practicable and easy, whether in ambush, in the open field, or while under the greatest speed on horseback.

The firing bolt is so adjusted that the hammer cannot possibly come in contact with it until the breech is perfectly closed, and the operator protected from injury by any accidental discharge. By depressing the lever the firing-bolt is automatically moved rearward by a spur or tooth on its forward end, which moves from a niche in the inner plane of the receiver, so far as to clear the bolt-point from the shell of the cartridge and the rear end of the barrel.

The exploded shell is thrown entirely clear of the arm by disengaging the hand from the lever as it passes over the centre.

These weapons have withstood the severest tests that Boards of Ordnance could subject them to. Among others, that of firing *three hundred rounds without wiping*, the last ten shots being at a target for accuracy.

Major General Hawley (since Governor of Connecticut, and now Member of Congress), wrote, Nov. 27, 1863, from St. Helena Island, South Carolina:

"Sharps Rifle is the best made arm that I have seen in the service. Ours have been now about twenty-six and a half months in the hands of the men, nearly all the time, *right by*, and sometimes in salt water, and they are in excellent condition. They have refuted, by actual tests, in battle and in camp, the objections so frequently made by old-fashioned people against breech-loading weapons."

Respectfully, your obedient servant,

JOSEPH R. HAWLEY.

The Company have, also, among many others, letters giving the most unqualified assurances of the merits of these arms from the following General, Field, Staff, and Line Officers, who served in the late war in the United States:

GENERAL W. T. SHERMAN,
LIEUT. GEN. SHERIDAN,

Major General	Robert Anderson,	Col.	T. Wolford,	1st Ky. Cav.
"	D. C. Buell,	"	Jackson, 3d	"
"	Rosecrans,	"	Bayles, 4th	"
"	Thomas,	"	Cooper, 4th	"
"	McCook,	"	Haggard, 5th	"
"	Nelson,	"	Watkins, 6th	"
"	Crittenden,	"	Shackleford, 8th	" Bt. B. Gen.
"	Gilbert,	"	Bristow, 8th	"
"	Granger,	"	Holloway, 8th	"
"	Smith,	"	E. M. McCook, 2d Ind. Cav. B.B.G.	
"	Wood,	"	Stewart, " "	
"	Howard,	"	Kennett, 4th Ohio Cavalry.	
"	Stanley,	"	Wynkoop, 7th Penn. Cavalry.	
"	Schofield,	"	Williams, 9th "	
"	Rosseau,	"	Berdan, Sharpshooters.	

Maj. General Palmer,
" Davis,
" Hooker,
" Slocum,
" McPherson,
" Butler,
" Hancock,
" Meade,
" Burnside,
" Custar,
" McLarnard,
" Logan,
" Steadman,
" Merritt,
" Heintzleman,
" Robinson,
" Terry,
Brigadier General Morgan,
" Schoff,
" R. S. Granger,
" Judah,
" Gillman,
" Bramlett,
" Burbridge,
" D. McCook,
" R. McCook,
" Van Cleave,
" Murray
" Mott, of New York,
" Brannar,
" Pry,
" Manson,
" Smith,
" Crupt,
" Boyle,
" Shackleford,
" Hobson,
" Terry, of Michigan,
" Whitaker,
" Farnsworth.

Col. McGowan, Berdan Sharpshooters.
" Fenke, "
" Ross, 20th Connecticut.
" Slocum, 2d Rhode Island.
Lt. Col. King.
" Moore.
Major Clay.
" Murray.
" Shacklett.
" Thomas, 1st Veteran Cavalry.
" Wolfley.
" Braithett.
" White.
" Alston, 3d N. J. Cavalry.
Captain McMurdy, 41st New York.
" Shister, 2d Penn. Cavalry.
" Cummings.
" Joniett.
Col. E. E.Cross,New Hampshire Vols.
" Leonidas Metcalf, KentuckyVols.
" Hurlburt E. Payne, 4th Wis. Vols.
" Gillman Marston, 2d N. H. Vols.
" H. A. V. Post, 2d Sharpshooters.
Lt. Col. S. C. Griffin, N. H. Vols.
Major C. H. Larabee, Wis. Vols.
" J. I. Dimock, 2d N. Y. S. Militia.
Capt. Charles S. Watrous, 76th N. Y.
" J. W. Carr, 2d New Hampshire.
" B. Giroux, Sharpshooters.
" J. B. Brookland, 9th Penn.
" E. P. Darlington, 9th Penn,
" W. T. Partridge, 5th N. Y.
" C. H. Craig, 105th Penn.
" George Charpenning,Penn Rifles.
" Ed. A. Hamilton,Sacramento S.S.
" Ira Wright, Ira Harris Cavalry.
" Milton B. Pierce, Sharpshooters.
" H. Bowen, Jr., 151st N. Y.
" A. E. Niles, 1st Penn. Rifles.
" Wm. D. Glass, 6th Ill. Cav.

Very important modifications and improvements (which have been patented), have been recently adopted by the Company, and these arms now stand, in every respect, pre-eminently ahead of any others made.

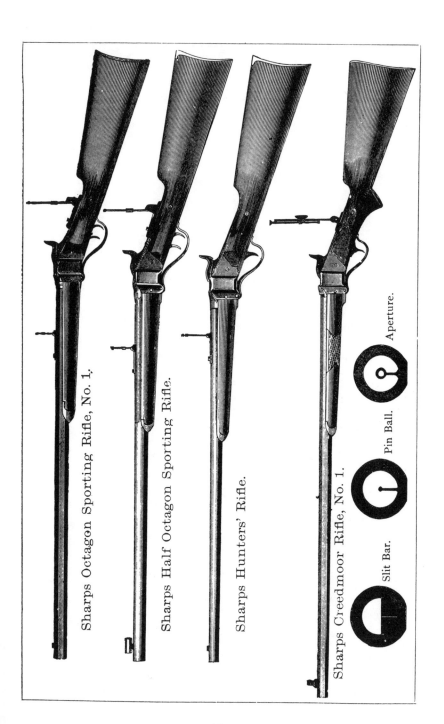

Sharps Octagon Sporting Rifle, No. 1.

Sharps Half Octagon Sporting Rifle.

Sharps Hunters' Rifle.

Sharps Creedmoor Rifle, No. 1.

Aperture.

Pin Ball.

Slit Bar.

Sharps Sporting

AND

CREEDMOOR RIFLES.

The Sharps Rifle Company have been compelled, by increased and constantly increasing demand for their productions, to largely extend their works, and are now prepared to fill orders promptly. These Rifles have stood the test of more than twenty years service in the hands of men whose lives depend upon the accuracy and powerful qualities of their weapons, and are to-day universally prized by hunters, trappers, frontiersmen and sportsmen generally.

For Safety, Accuracy, Simplicity and Penetration,

COMBINED WITH UNEQUALLED WORKMANSHIP, THEY STAND UNRIVALED.

Every part is carefully and thoroughly inspected, each barrel is severely tested for accuracy and strength, and no work that is not as

ABSOLUTELY PERFECT

as human skill and experience can produce, is permitted to leave the Armory.

In using this weapon the hunter or marksman cannot be injured by accidental discharge while loading, the Sharps in this respect possessing a virtue shared by few other breech loaders. The exploded shell is always infallibly removed by the lever.

At the Creedmoor Range, near New York city, in the Summer of 1873, the Sharps Rifle made the following record:

Winner of the Amateur Club Gold Medal for 500 yards, three times, with scores of 26, 27, 28, against 25, 27, 25, 28, by other rifles. Winner's average with Sharps 27 out of a possible 28. Winner's average with other rifles, 26, 25.

Winner of four out of six prizes in the match for military rifles at 500 yards, June 6th. Winner's average with Sharps Military Rifles, 25, 25. Winner's average with other rifles, 24, 50.

Match for the Amateur Club, Saturday, June 20th.

Distances 800, 900 *and* 1,000 *yards.*

Nine Sharps and ten *other* rifles entered. Sharps won the gold medal. Average, 25.88 and average for the *others*, 23.50. Odds in favor of Sharps Rifles *over two and one-third points per man.*

Match of same club, same distance, June 28th, eight Sharps and ten *other* rifles entered. Average for Sharps 28.37. Average for the *other*, 23.77. Odds gained by using Sharps 4.60.

Match for Turf, Field and Farm Badge, same day, 200 yards off hand. Sharps average 13.80. The others 12.35.

WON DIAMOND BADGE Saturday, July 11, at 500, 800 and 1000 yards, making score of 71 out of a possible 84.

In the International Match at Creedmoor, September, 1874, between the Irish and American teams, (won by the Americans), the Sharps Long Range Rifle made the highest score of any breech loader used as such, at 800, 900 and 1,000 yards, (see Target printed on another page) and on the same range, one week later, The Sharps Rifle Company were the only American manufacturers who dared accept the challenge of Mr. J. Rigby, of the Irish team, for a test of breech loaders against muzzle loaders, twenty-five rounds each, at 1,000 yards, *without wiping.* Here, also, the Sharps proved its great superiority.

At the Fall Meeting, beginning Sept. 29th, 1874, of the National Rifle Association, at Creedmoor, the SHARPS RIFLE won the following prizes:

ARMY AND NAVY JOURNAL MATCH.

500 yards. Open to teams from all regularly organized Military organizations in the United States—180 entries—*only 12 Sharps Rifles used.*

FIRST PRIZE, Silver plate, value $750.00.
SECOND PRIZE, Silver cup, value $50.00.

The Sharps Rifle, also, won in this match the First and four other of eight prizes given for the best individual scores.

NOTE.—The Seventh New York Regiment, whose team won the First Prize, $750.00 in this match, are armed with Remington Rifles, but a majority of the team laid aside their own rifles and used the SHARPS.

Of the team of the Twelfth New York Regiment (also armed with Remington Rifles), that won the second prize, (Cup, value $50.00), five men out of the twelve used the SHARPS Rifle in preference to their own weapons.

ALL COMERS' MATCH.

500 and 600 yards. 12 prizes in all—200 Entries. The Sharps Rifle won the 1st, 2nd, 3rd, 4th and three others, (in all 7 out of 12).

PRESS MATCH.

500 yards. The Sharps Rifle won first prize, Gold medal, value $50.00 ; also, 2nd, 7th and 9th prizes.

BENNETT MATCH.

800, 900 and 1,000 yards. The Sharps Rifle won 13 prizes.

————◆◆————

Weight of Rifles, 8 to 12 lbs. Charge of Powder, 50 to 95 grains. Length of Ball, $\frac{7}{8}$, $1\frac{1}{8}$, $1\frac{1}{4}$, $1\frac{3}{8}$ inches. Caliber, $\frac{40}{100}$ — $\frac{44}{100}$ — $\frac{45}{100}$ — $\frac{50}{100}$.

PRICE LIST.

In making prices for their arms, The Sharps Rifle Company make no attempt to compete with other and inferior manufacturers. Only skilled labor and the best materials are employed in their works, and the high reputation and intrinsic excellence of their productions are thus always maintained.

THE BEST ALWAYS THE CHEAPEST.

SHARPS SPORTING RIFLES.

Weight, 8 to 12 lbs. $\frac{40}{100}$—$\frac{44}{100}$—$\frac{45}{100}$ and $\frac{50}{100}$ caliber, polished stock, open sights, single trigger.

26 in. Octagon Barrel, - $35 00	26 in. Half Octagon Barrel, $33 00
28 " " - - 36 50	28 " " " 34 50
30 " " - - 38 00	30 " " " 36 00

SHARPS HUNTERS' RIFLES.

Weight 8 to 10 lbs. $\frac{40}{100}$--$\frac{44}{100}$—$\frac{45}{100}$ and $\frac{50}{100}$ caliber, oiled stock, plain finish, open sights, single trigger.

26 inch Round Barrel, - - $30 00
28 " " " - - - 31 50
30 " " " - - 33 00

SHARPS CREEDMOOR RIFLES.

Patched balls are invariably used with these arms, with lubricating material, that prevents entirely the fouling or leading of the barrel, thereby securing a reliable and accurate shooting rifle for long ranges.

SHARPS CREEDMOOR RIFLE No. 4.

$\frac{44}{100}$ caliber, 30 inch barrel, regular hunting, polished stock, under 10 lbs. weight, globe, peep and open sights, with elevation sufficient for 1,000 yards. Designed for long range, target or hunting, - - - - $65 00

SHARPS CREEDMOOR RIFLE No. 3.

$\frac{44}{100}$ caliber, 30 inch barrel, hand-made polished stock, with broad, flat butt, under 10 lbs. weight, globe, peep, and open sights, with elevation sufficient for 1,000 yards, **$75 00**

SHARPS CREEDMOOR RIFLE No. 2.

$\frac{44}{100}$ caliber, 32 inch barrel, long, straight, hand-made, polished stock, weight just under 10 lbs., trigger pull 3 lbs., peep, rear sight, with Vernier scale, by means of which a register may be kept of the elevation required for a given distance under varying circumstances; wind gauge, with interchangeable globe and split-bar front sights, - - - - - - - - **$90 00**

SHARPS CREEDMOOR RIFLE No. 1.

Designed exclusively for very long ranges. $\frac{44}{100}$ caliber, 32 inch barrel, long, straight, hand-made *pistol grip*, polished stock, checkered grip and fore-end, regulation weight and trigger pull; peep, rear sight, with Vernier scale, allowing the necessary elevation for 1,300 yards ; wind gauge, with interchangeable globe and split bar front sight, with morocco sight case. (This is the very best rifle manufactured, and will be found to give splendid results at the longest ranges), - - - - **$125 00**

Spirit level attached to front sight, extra, - -

Special arms of any weight, length, or caliber, made or engraved to order at the armory.

Globe and Peep Sights, extra,	-	-	-	$5 00
Double Triggers, "		-	-	- 4 00
Telescope Sights, "		-	-	- 40 00

CARTRIDGES.

$\frac{40}{100}$ caliber, centre fire, reloading shells, 50 grains powder, naked ball (2 cannelures), weight 246 grains, per 1,000 **$40 00**

$\frac{44}{100}$ caliber, centre fire, reloading shells, 70 grains powder, naked ball (2 cannelures), weight 312 grains, per 1,000 **$42 00**

Same with patched ball, 380 grains, - per 1,000, $45 00
     "   "   "   422   " - -   "   45 00

$\frac{50}{100}$ caliber, centre fire, re-loading shells, 70 grains powder,

     naked ball (3 cannelures), weight 457 grains, per 1,000   42 00

Same, with smooth, patched ball, weight, 500 grains, per 1,000   45 00

Ball Swedges, all sizes and calibers, to order.

BRASS, CENTRE FIRE RE-LOADING SHELLS.

$\frac{40}{100}$ Caliber,	$1\frac{11}{16}$ inches long,	-	-		per 1,000		$22 00
$\frac{40}{100}$ "	$2\frac{1}{4}$ "	-	-	-	"		24 00
$\frac{40}{100}$ "	$2\frac{5}{8}$ "	-	-	-	"		30 00
$\frac{44}{100}$ "	$2\frac{1}{4}$ "	-	-	-	"		26 50
$\frac{44}{100}$ "	$2\frac{5}{8}$ "	-	-	-	"		32 00
$\frac{45}{100}$ "	$2\frac{1}{4}$ "	-	-	-	"		26 50
$\frac{45}{100}$ "	$2\frac{5}{8}$ "	-	-	-	"		32 00
$\frac{50}{100}$ "	$1\frac{3}{4}$ "	-	-	-	"		22 00
$\frac{50}{100}$ "	2 "	-	-	-	"		24 00
$\frac{50}{100}$ "	$2\frac{1}{4}$ "	-	•	•	"		30 00

With proper care in re-loading these shells may be used for an almost indefinite number of firings. In testing them at the armory, single shells have been re-loaded and fired as high as *five hundred times* without rendering them useless.

Sharps Powder,   -   -   -   -   per lb. $1 00
Lubricating Disks,   ·   -   -   -   per 1,000,   1 25
     "   Material,   -   -   -   per lb.   1 25
Ball Moulds, Sporting,   -   -   -   -   3 00
     "   "   Creedmoor,   -   -   -   -   4 00
Wad Cutters,   -   -   -   -   -   0 75
Cap Awls,   -   -   -   -   -   -   0 25
Lubricating Moulds,   -   ··   -   -   -   0 50
Ball Seaters,   -   -   -   -   -   -   1 00
Followers,   -   -   ··   -   -   -   0 50

Score Books, for keeping diagrams of targets, records of
     scores, elevations of sights, and variations of wind
     gauge, classified in a simple manner,   -   -   - $0 50

CASES FOR RIFLES.

Black Walnut (lined),	-	-	each $7 00 to $15 00
Mahogany, "	-	-	" 7 50 to 20 00
Rosewood, "	-	-	" 20 00 to 40 00
Russet Leather (stiff), Trunk Shape,	-	-	15 00
" " " Gun Shape,	-	-	5 00
Bag Leather, Flexible, Gun Shape,	-	-	3 00
Sheepskin,	-	-	2 00
Canvas,	-	-	2 50
Cartridge Belts,	-	-	5 00
Cartridge Box and Belt,	-	-	1 25

Goods will be forwarded from the armory to any part of the country, by express, with bill to collect on delivery. Persons not known to the company are required to remit by Post-office order, draft on New York, or otherwise, at least one-fourth of the probable cost of the goods ordered, as an evidence of their good faith.

Arrangements have been made with the different Express Companies for special minimum rates on all matter forwarded from The Sharps Rifle Company.

INSTRUCTIONS

FOR

RE-LOADING METALLIC SHELLS

ISSUED WITH

SHARPS RIFLES AND CARBINES.

The cartridges issued with the Sharps Company's Arms are made up of shells that are susceptible of being re-loaded and fired many times.

After the cartridge has been fired, the following process must be strictly observed in re-loading :

Bore a hole in a piece of hard wood, the size of the body of the cartridge, leaving the rim of the cartridge even with the surface of the board, in which place the empty shell.

Perforate the exploded cap on one side of its centre with the awl, and pry out the exploded cap; clean out the debris in the small end of the shell perfectly, and insert a new cap in the head of the shell, setting it home snugly by pressure.

Charge with 70 grains of powder, with a pasteboard wad upon the powder, forcing the wad down the full length of the follower.

Insert upon the wad a lubricant disk composed of one part of pure beeswax to 2 parts sperm oil in weight, to occupy 3-16 of an inch in length in the shell.

Dip the base of the ball up to the forward ring in the melted lubricating compound, taking care to fill the grooves.

Insert the point of the ball in the chamber of the Ball Seater, and introduce the shell through the circular orifice at the opposite end of the Ball Seater, and press the shell home with the hand or a soft piece of wood.

Wipe the cartridge clean and it is ready for use.

In re-loading with patched ball, the Ball Seater is not used ; the ball is seated with the hands.

In casting balls, first heat your moulds nearly as hot as the molten lead, having cleaned them of all oily substance.

DIRECTIONS FOR CLEANING, ETC.

Clean your arm and its parts with a rag moistened with oil; water is unnecessary, and may be injurious.

To detach the lever, breech-pin, and extractor, throw down the lever, depress the small spur contiguous to the arm of the lever-pin in the right-hand side of the breech-piece, and swing the arm of the lever-pin a half turn, withdrawing it, and the parts are released.

To replace them, put the three parts in the same relative position as they occupied when the lever-pin was being removed, and they will readily move to place and be secured by the lever-pin.

The barrel should be brushed or wiped from the rear end, a very decided advantage that our arm possesses over all others, that clean only from the muzzle, and eject the debris into the working parts at the breech.

SHARPS IMPROVED

CREEDMOOR RIFLES.

DIRECTIONS FOR RE-LOADING CARTRIDGE SHELLS.

Replace the exploded cap with a new one; load with 90 grains American Powder Co.'s "Sharps Powder," specially manufactured for The Sharps Rifle Company. Place a thin wad on the Powder, press the wad home with the follower; then put a Lubricant Disk, composed of Sperm Oil and Beeswax, on the wad; and the shell is ready to receive the ball, which is placed in position with the hand.

ELEVATIONS FOR LONG RANGES.

The elevation of the rear aperture sight for each distance is obtained by moving the screw until the scale indicates the number of hundredths of an inch, given in the annexed table.

The main scale is graduated in equal decimals of 10ths and 20ths of an inch. The slide has a short Vernier scale which will enable any one to count hundredths of an inch. The bottom line of this scale is that used in measuring the elevations; the others serve to enable the shooter to move the slide $\frac{1}{100}$ of an inch at a time when necessary. The front sight or wind gauge is graduated in 40ths of an inch, equal to about 2 inches for every 100 yards.

SCALE OF ELEVATIONS.

For 200 yards,	-	-	.11	For 700 yards,	-	-	.92
" 300 yards,	-	-	- .25	" 800 yards,	-	-	- 1.10
" 400 yards,	-	-	.40	" 900 yards,	-	-	1.30
" 500 yards,	-	-	- .57	" 1000 yards,	-	-	- 1.51
" 600 yards,	-	-	.74	" 1100 yards,	-	-	1.73

This is an *average* table for a $\frac{44}{100}$ caliber rifle, with a cartridge of 90 grains of powder and 500 grains of lead. Any change in the cartridge necessitates a change in the elevations, and any sportsman will easily learn to adjust the scale of his own rifle.

In order to secure reliable and accurate shooting with a breech-loading rifle, the same nice care of ammunition must be exercised as with a muzzle loader. After many years experience, and many experiments, this company have succeeded, beyond a question, in producing arms and ammunition that will give entire satisfaction.

Our arms do not foul or lead with ammunition made up at the armory, and we cannot insure them to do good shooting unless ammunition is used which is made up under our special instructions in every particular.

All experts are aware that, in order to insure good shooting, it is absolutely necessary to use large charges of powder, and that light balls, with heavy charges, make low trajectory lines only at short ranges, and by increasing length of ball much lower lines are made at long ranges with the same charge of powder.

All arms are made with special reference to use the light, naked or heavy, smooth, patched ball, with the same charge of powder which is adapted to each size shell and caliber.

TESTIMONIALS.

The following are a few extracts, selected almost at random from a multitude of letters of commendation received by the Company' from persons who are using the improved Sporting and Long Range Rifles. Of the thousands who have recently purchased, they have yet to hear of one who is dissatisfied :

From J. A. MELVIN, *Ellis, Kansas, July* 12, 1871.

"The gun is received. It is a good gun as far as tried, and suits me to a dot."

From R. W. SNYDER, *Buffalo, Kansas, November* 20, 1871.

"The gun, I must say, is a success,—and the Pet of the Plains,—in fact, has no equal, to my knowledge. I killed twelve Buffalo with it in thirteen shots, the third day after it arrived, which is much better than I have ever done with any other gun."

From R. W. SNYDER, Esq., *Buffalo, Kansas, December* 18, 1872.

"The man that I sold my old 44 to, killed 119 Buffalo, in one day, with it. That beats me with my big 50,—as 93 is the most that I have ever killed in one day."

From IRVIN A. FIST, *North Platte, Nebraska, February*, 22, 1872.

"Having been a frontier man, and followed the profession of Hunter for some years past, I find your rifle to surpass any in use at the present time on the Plains. Its heavy charge of Powder and small Caliber, with heavy ball, enable us to shoot Antelopes, and others which are watchful and hard to approach, at greater distance than any other Rifle now in use."

From W. C. ALDERSON, *Philadelphia, February* 23, 1872.

"I have tested your Rifle lately, both with the sample ammunition you sent me, and also with some prepared by myself after your directions, and can say that I am very much pleased with its performance, although I tried it under the disadvantage of a cold day and high wind."

From W. COOPER, Esq., *Bozeman, Montana, April* 9, 1872.

"Those four guns you sent me take the eye of every one. They outshoot anything ever brought to this country. I won a bet of ten dollars the other day on penetration against an army musket,—called the Springfield Needle Gun here. Shot the same powder and shot two inches deeper into wood."

From H. P. WEAVER, *Findley's Lake, N. Y., May* 22, 1872.

"I have had my gun long enough now to know how I like it, and I now write to let you know that it is the best Rifle that I ever drew to my face, and that is saying a good deal, for I have shot some splendid Rifles. It is the longest range and the most accurate shooting Rifle I ever saw. Every one that has seen it shot, says that its equal has not been made."

Sharps Rifle Co.,

BRIDGEPORT, CONN.,

ORGANIZED AT HARTFORD, CONN., OCT. 9, 1851. U. S. A. REMOVED TO BRIDGEPORT, CONN., FEB. 1, 1876.

MANUFACTURERS OF

Sharps Patent Breech-Loading, Metallic Cartridge Military Rifles and Carbines, Match Rifles, &c.

(Old Reliable)

(TRADE MARK.)

The Sharps system of Breech-loading Arms was invented in 1848 by Christian Sharps, and was the first successful breech-loader made. The manufacture of these arms was begun on a large scale at Hartford, Conn., in 1851, by the Sharps' Rifle Manufacturing Co., and continued for many years with unprecedented success, and until the Company became involved in litigation with an associate, which was long prosecuted with much acrimony on both sides. Finally, in 1875, worn out by the expenses and delays of these suits, (during the progress of which their production of arms had almost ceased,) and unable to effect any satisfactory adjustment of their differences, all the parties in interest united in a sale of the old Company's effects to a new organization, specially chartered by the State of Connecticut, with an authorized capital of one million dollars. The original company consequently dissolved and went out of existence.

This new organization, under the name of **SHARPS RIFLE COMPANY**, at once began at Bridgeport, Conn., (a manufacturing centre, ninety minutes by rail from New York city) the erection of a new armory containing about 90,000 superficial feet of working room, to which they removed in January, 1876, and are now prepared to execute contracts for arms in quantities.

During the twelve years of inaction of the original company it retained the services of Mr. R. S. LAWRENCE, an inventor and practical manufacturer of national celebrity, who thus had ample opportunity to experiment upon and improve the arm, which had already, under his supervision, distanced all competitors.

SHARPS MILITARY RIFLES AND CARBINES are confidently recommended

1st. For their strength, simplicity and durability. So simple is its construction that rapid loading is easy, whether in the open field, in ambush, or at the greatest speed on horseback.

2d. The ease with which the several parts can be kept clean and in working order. The barrel is open to instant and unobstructed inspection, and can be brushed or wiped from the breech, thus ejecting the debris from the muzzle—a decided advantage over those that can only be wiped from the muzzle, throwing the debris into the working parts.

3d. Their accuracy at short, mid and long ranges.

4th. Their perfect safety.

This Rifle has been before a critical public for over 25 years, and although Hundreds of Thousands of them have been sold to Soldiers, Hunters, Sportsmen, Rifle Clubs, and others, yet no instance has occurred of injury inflicted through any defect of system, workmanship or material.

5th. The rapidity and uniformity of their fire. Fifteen rounds *at aim* with the ordinary arm, and a much greater number with the self-cocking model, are easily fired in one minute. Ten seconds is ample time for cleaning after having fired 100 rounds.

The firing-bolt is so adjusted that the hammer cannot possibly come in contact with it until the breech is perfectly closed, and the operator protected from injury by any accidental discharge. By depressing the lever the firing-bolt is automatically moved rearward by a spur or tooth on its forward end, which moves from a niche in the inner plane of the receiver, so far as to clear the bolt-point from the shell of the cartridge and the rear end of the barrel.

The exploded shell is thrown entirely clear of the arm by disengaging the hand from the lever as it passes over the centre.

A patent has recently been obtained for an improvement by which in either opening or closing the breech the hammer is automatically raised into the safety notch, so that it is impracticable to load the arm except while at half-cock.

The SHARPS RIFLE was subjected to the following severe tests by a Board of Officers of the U. S. Army, (see Report of Chief of Ordnance, U. S. A., 1873) in each of which, without a single failure, it triumphantly sustained its reputation.

SAFETY TEST : To be fired 10 rounds by the exhibitor, or with a Lanyard.

I. DEFECTIVE CARTRIDGES.—Each gun to be fired once with each of the following defective cartridges. 1. Cross-filed on head to nearly the thickness of the metal. 2. Cut at intervals around the rim. 3. With a longitudinal cut the whole length of the cartridge from the rim up. A fresh piece of white paper marked with the number of the gun being laid over the breech to observe the escape of gas, if any occurs.

II. RAPIDITY WITH ACCURACY.—The number of shots which, fired in one minute, strike a target 6 feet by 2 feet at a distance of 100 feet. Any cartridge missing fire in this or other tests to be tried with a prick-punch, or opened to ascertain the cause of failure. The test to be begun with an empty chamber or magazine, the cartridges to be disposed at will on a table.

III. RAPIDITY AT WILL.—The number of shots which can be fired in one minute, irrespective of aim.

IV. ENDURANCE.—Each gun to be fired 500 continuous rounds without cleaning. The state of the breech mechanism to be examined at the end of every 50 rounds.

V. DUST.—The piece to be exposed in the box prepared for that purpose to a blast of fine sand-dust for 2 minutes; to be removed, fired 20 rounds, replaced for 2 minutes, removed and fired 20 rounds more.

VI. RUST.—The breech mechanism and receiver to be cleansed of grease and the chamber of the barrel greased and plugged, the butt of the gun to be inserted to the height of the chamber in a solution of sal-ammoniac for 10 minutes, exposed for two days to the open air standing in a rack, and then fired 20 rounds.

VII. EXCESSIVE CHARGES.—To be fired once with 85 grains of powder and one ball of 450 grains of lead; once with 90 grains and one ball; once with 90 grains and two balls, and once with 150 grains of powder and 1,200 grains of lead. The piece to be closely examined after each discharge.

It is worthy of note that at the close of the war **SHARPS RIFLES AND CARBINES** were the only arms of all the various breech-loaders purchased ·or made by the government that were retained and are now in use by the United States Army. All others, *without exception,* were sold or condemned and broken up.

The greatest care is taken that all Military Rifles made by the **SHARPS COMPANY** shall be perfect in their shooting qualities. At the Creedmoor Range, near New York city, **SHARPS MILITARY RIFLES** have won a long succession of victories over those of other manufacturers; and now, teams using the SHARPS RIFLES on that Range are handicapped with long odds, as an offset to the advantage they gain by the superiority of these arms over those of rival makers.

Only the very best MATERIAL is used, and the WORKMANSHIP of the product of SHARPS works is unexcelled in any armory in the world. Indeed, the U. S. Government, years ago, made the SHARPS WORKMANSHIP the standard for its armories.

The arms produced in the different periods of development of the SHARPS RIFLE have never failed to do excellent service, and of the great numbers made and sold to the different nations of the world, all have given the most unqualified satisfaction to the purchasers.

During the late civil war in the United States the SHARPS Works were kept fully employed by the government. Many regiments of volunteers made it one of the conditions of enlisting in the U. S. Army that they should be armed with SHARPS RIFLES. Gen. T. S. ELLIS, a distinguished officer, wrote from the field :

"The men are so confident of the superiority of SHARPS RIFLES, that they will at any time throw away their other weapons in action, to secure one dropped by a disabled comrade."

Major-Gen'l. HAWLEY, since Governor of Connecticut, and Member of Congress, now President of the U. S. Centennial Commission, wrote Nov. 27th, 1863, from St. Helena Island, South Carolina :

"SHARPS RIFLE is the best made arm that I have seen in the service. Ours have been now about twenty-six and a half months in the hands of the men, nearly all the time, *right by*, and sometimes in salt water, and they are in excellent condition."

The Company have among a host of others, letters giving the most unqualified assurances of the merits of these arms from the following General and Field Officers who served in the late war in the United States :

GENERAL W. T. SHERMAN,
LIEUT. GEN. SHERIDAN,

Major-General Robert Anderson,			Brigadier-Gen. Judah.
"	D. C. Buell,		" Gilman.
"	Rosecrans,		" Bramlett.
"	Thomas,		" Burbridge.
"	McCook,		" D. McCook.
"	Nelson,		" R. McCook.
"	Crittenden,		" Van Cleavh.
"	Gilbert,		" Murray.
"	Granger,		" Mott, of New York.
"	Smith,		" Brannan.
"	Wood,		" Pry,
"	Howard,		" Manson.
"	Stanley,		" Smith.
"	Schofield,		" Crupt.
"	Rousseau,		" Doyle.
"	Palmer,		" Shackleford.
"	Davis,		" Hobson.
"	Hooker,		" Terry, of Michigan.
"	Slocum,		" Whitaker.
"	McP'herson,		" Farnsworth.
"	Butler,	Col. T. Wolford,	1st Ky. Cav.
"	Hancock,	" Jackson,	3d "
"	Meade,	" Bayles,	4th "
"	Burnside,	" Cooper,	4th "
"	Custar,	" Haggard,	5th "
"	McLarnard,	" Watkins,	6th "
"	Logan,	" Shackleford,	8th "
"	Steadman,	" Bristow,	8th "
"	Merritt,	" Holloway,	8th "
"	Heintzleman,	" E. M. McCook,	2d Indiana Cav., Bvt. Brig. Gen.
"	Robinson,	" Stewart,	" " "
"	Terry,	" Kennett,	4th Ohio Cavalry.
Brigadier-Gen. Morgan,		" Wynkoop,	7th Penn. Cavalry.
"	Schoff,	" Williams,	9th "
"	R. S. Granger.	" Berdan,	Sharpshooters. •

Soldiers, Hunters, and Marksmen have, as their estimate of its excellent qualities, long given the name of "**Old Reliable**," to the SHARPS RIFLE, and the Company have adopted that as their Trade Mark, which will hereafter appear upon all of their productions.

BRIDGEPORT, Conn., April 25, 1876.

Old Reliable

(TRADE MARK.)

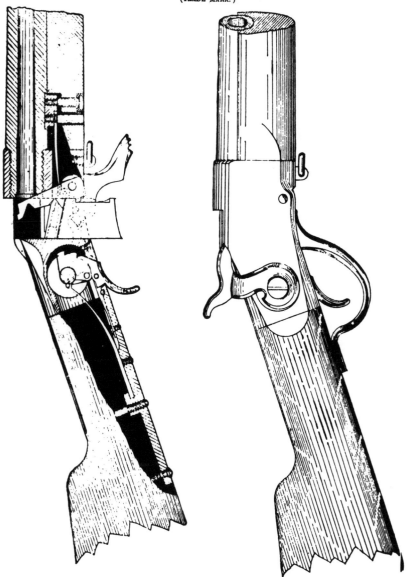

MODEL 1875.

SHARPS
RIFLE COMPANY,

BRIDGEPORT, CONN.,

U. S. A

> OLD RELIABLE.
>
> [Trade Mark.]

MANUFACTURERS OF PATENT

BREECH LOADING FIRE ARMS

AND

AMMUNITION.

NEW YORK CITY WAREROOMS, 177 BROADWAY.

E. G. WESTCOTT,

President.

CHAS. H. POND,

Secretary.

SPECIAL ANNOUNCEMENT!

SHARPS DOUBLE-BARRELED SHOT-GUN.

The trade, and our friends generally throughout the country, have long urged us to make a shot gun that should equal the Sharps Rifle in excellence, and which, at the same time, could be sold at a price within the reach of the great majority of the American people. We have decided to meet this want, and have now in preparation the machinery and tools for its manufacture. We expect to be ready to fill orders about May 1st.

SHARPS RIFLE COMPANY,

Bridgeport, Conn.

ARMORY OF SHARPS RIFLE CO.,
Bridgeport, Conn., U. S. A.

January, 1878.

N presenting to the public its new price list, the SHARPS RIFLE Co. takes occasion to thank its customers and friends for their continued favors, and congratulates them upon the improved business prospects for the coming year in all branches of trade. The indications are that the demand for SHARPS RIFLES will be unprecedented; it has already necessitated increased facilities for manufacture. This is largely due to the fact that the Company has strictly adhered to its practice of using only the best obtainable material, and employing only the most skillful workmen, which policy will be rigidly adhered to. No work that is not perfect is permitted to leave the armory; every piece is carefully and thoroughly inspected, and each barrel is severely tested for accuracy and strength. Many improvements have been made during the past year, more especially in the breech action, which has been lightened without impairing its strength, and the cumbrous hammer (relic of the flint-lock) done away with. More particular descriptions, with illustrations, will be found in succeeding pages. The long range rifle has maintained its claims to wear (with all products of the armory) the legend " Old Reliable." In computing percentages made in the great International Match of 1876 with forty competitors in the field, using rifles of six different makers including all the *crack* British muzzle loaders, it was found that SHARPS headed the list with .877, the next highest scoring only .867. (See official report in *Rod and Gun*, September 30, 1876.) In the International Match of 1877, America against best marksmen of England, Ireland, and Scotland, in spite of tremendous efforts of other manufacturers to get to the front, SHARPS is found still leading the van with an average of 420 per man against 414 by any other rifle, and a percentage of .933, the next highest being but .920. Still further improvements have been made in the model for 1878, and the Company feels warranted in claiming that for accuracy and other merits it will be unapproached by any other arm. The improved action has been applied to the military rifle, and the arm otherwise so advanced that they feel confident that their claim that it is the "*best in the world*" cannot be controverted. Although it was very late in the season before the first few samples were made, yet orders are already pouring in from all directions. It is recommended in the highest terms by all military men who have examined it.

The history of SHARPS Rifle is generally well known, but it may be briefly stated that it was invented in 1848, and was the first successful breech loader ever made. A company for its manufacture was organized at Hartford, Conn., in 1851, which carried on the business there for many years with very great success. In 1875, a new company was formed with its present title, under a special charter from the State of Connecticut, with an authorized capital of one million dollars. Early in 1876, the new organization erected an armory at Bridgeport, Conn. (a manufacturing centre, ninety minutes by rail from New York), where it has about 90,000 superficial feet of working room upon a site of twenty-two acres, on the line of the N. Y., N. H. & H. R.R., with navigable water on the premises, and with every facility in the way of machinery and tools for turning out the best of work.

SHARPS RIFLES of all descriptions are specially noted for the following qualities:

I. SAFETY.—Although hundreds of thousands have been in use during the past thirty years by soldiers, hunters, sportsmen, and others, yet no instance has occurred of injury through any defect of system, workmanship, or material.

II. ACCURACY.—See the records of all the great rifle matches and the testimony of experts and celebrated shots, nearly all of whom use the SHARPS arms.

III. DURABILITY —Large numbers of the Rifles made in 1852

and '3 are still in use, and apparently as good as ever.   [It is worthy of note that at the close of the late "unpleasantness," SHARPS RIFLES AND CARBINES were the only arms of all the various breech-loaders purchased or made by the Government that were retained and are now in use by the United States Army.   All others, *without exception*, were sold, or condemned and broken up.]   Gen'l Steele, who used SHARPS RIFLES on the Texas frontier for many years, reports that he never had occasion to send one to the gunsmith for repairs.

IV. The ease with which the several parts can be kept clean and in working order.—The barrel is open to instant and unobstructed inspection, and can be brushed or wiped from the breech, thus ejecting the debris from the muzzle – a decided advantage over those that can only be wiped from the muzzle, throwing the debris into the working parts. The judges of rifles at the Centennial Exhibition, told the whole story in three short words, as follows:

INTERNATIONAL EXHIBITION,

PHILADELPHIA, 1876.

Judges' report on SHARPS Breech-loading Rifles:
" Simple, Strong, and Good."

A true copy of the record,

FRANCIS A. WALKER,

Chief of Bureau of Awards.

OPINIONS OF THE PRESS.

"Old Reliable."

For a few weeks past the sound which has attracted the greatest attention in either hemisphere has been the crack of the rifle. In the Shipka Pass it has been the death-knell of thousands upon thousands of men who have slaughtered, and in their turn been slaughtered, till the heart of the world is sick at the carnage. In our own land thousands have also hung breathless upon the gun's report, but here the sound has had nothing of menace about it. Deadly and relentless accuracy has been displayed, but with us the unerring lead has flattened itself harmlessly against plates of iron, instead of cleaving human hearts as before the walls of Plevna.

Surely "Peace hath her victories no less renowned than war," and the grand Creedmoor meeting of 1877 has witnessed one of these which is already historical. Greek met Greek when the British and American rifle teams struggled for the Centennial trophy throughout the days of the 13th and 14th inst., and while, with such shooting as was then exhibited, defeat itself was an honor, the victory which rewarded the magnificent efforts of the Americans was glory indeed.

This never-to-be-forgotten contest has proved the SHARPS improved long range rifle to be the most perfect arm the world ever saw, and has made it the acknowledged standard. Bruce, the hero of the American team, who, on the last day, made the unheard-of record, 219 out of a possible 225, used this wonderful gun, and, at the conclusion of the match made the emphatic remark "That SHARPS Rifle made my record; I only happened to be behind it." Most convincing testimony is the action of the British marksmen—seven of whom have bought the SHARPS for their own future use. Among this seven is Wm. Rigby, of Wm. & John Rigby, Dublin, now and for many years the most celebrated rifle makers of Great Britain. If anything more than its record were needed to show the shooting world that they *must* use the SHARPS gun hereafter to stand any show, it strikes us this episode furnishes it.

This last circumstance is really a most remarkable one. That the Englishman should so thoroughly and unconditionally "acknowledge the corn" must surprise any one who knows the sturdy and often unreasoning patriotism which is their foremost national characteristic, and which, in connection with their conceded and highly prized precedence in skillful and athletic sports generally, must have made this forced admission of American superiority a bitter pill.

The SHARPS Rifle, which is now by common consent the standard rifle of the world, is the result of more than a quarter of a century's invention and improvement, culminating in the final modification of the firing action, made during the past summer. The original gun was invented in 1848 by CHRISTIAN SHARPS, who was practically the founder of the breech-loading system.

Its manufacture was commenced on a large scale in 1851, at Hartford, Conn., and for several years was carried on with the greatest success. The weapon presented such obvious advantages over anything previously attempted that it became a favorite on sight, and was introduced into the armies of so many governments, our own included, that the capacity of the Company was taxed to the utmost. But litigation finally sprung up to interfere with this splendid prosperity, and was so bitter and so prolonged that the production of their guns was almost entirely suspended for some years. In 1875, however, all parties to the suit agreed to merge their interests, and a new company having been formed under the name of SHARPS Rifle Company, with an authorized capital of $1,000,000, all old difficulties were removed, and active operations were recommenced with the utmost vigor. Bridgeport, Conn., was fixed upon as a permanent location, and here the Company erected the immense armory which they now occupy.

But although, as above stated, manufacture was interrupted during a term of years, it must not be inferred that the Company was idle. Experiment and study were constantly busy with the gun, and when, therefore, the reorganization was effected, the Company found, ready to their hands, models not only up with the times in every respect, but as far in advance of competition in many points as was the original SHARPS at the time of its invention. But they did not stop here. Study and experiment were still continued, and as before indicated, have just brought about an important and highly satisfactory modification of the breech.

From personal examination and comparison, made since the Creedmoor match, we can emphatically and confidently state that the SHARPS rifles of to-day—military, sporting, and long range—are superior in model, in strength, in action, in simplicity, to any others made. As to their accuracy, we need say nothing, as that is a matter of record and not of opinion. In the first International match for the Centennial trophy, their percentage was .877 as compared with .867 of the Remington, and the far lower averages of the four British guns there used. This year it was 420 against 414 4-5 of all other rifles. Mr. Gilder, one of the British marksmen above referred to, carries home with him one of the new guns which, on its first trial at the factory, last week, made sixteen consecutive bullseyes at 1000 yards. It is this kind of work which has made the SHARPS trademark, "Old Reliable," accepted as a just description of its character. Quality of material and workmanship not being a subject for patent or invention, all first-class makers are, or may be, on a par in that respect. It goes without saying that the SHARPS are of the very finest in all points.

In appearance the SHARPS is as faultless as in working principle. From muzzle to shoulder-plate it is clean and clear of all projections save trigger and sights, the latest improvements having done away with the obsolete hammer, that clumsy and dangerous relic of the old flintlock, which a custom as obstinate as it is senseless has persisted in retaining until very lately, and substituted the safe and sensible horizontal firing-pin. This change is known as the Borchardt patent. The trigger is provided with an automatic check—a proper, though hardly necessary precaution, as there is no external hammer to be accidentally struck, and the firing mechanism is such that no amount of jarring will discharge the piece even when at full cock.

In view of the preceding, and various other considerations, we are convinced that the SHARPS Rifles are the best for all purposes. For military use this superiority is well-nigh unquestioned. For sporting and long range it has but one competitor worthy the name, and with regard to this one, apart from all question of accuracy or model the absolute safety of the SHARPS, and the absolute unsafeness of the latter, ought to be sufficient to settle the preference.

The Company is now filling an order to go to a foreign government, and have other large foreign orders in prospect.

—*New York Merchants' Journal*, Sept. 22, 1877.

The Rifle Victory.

Yesterday will ever be marked with a white stone among American riflemen. Their most sanguine hopes of success have been far exceeded. The day before, the highest point in rifle shooting had been reached by a total of 1,655 in a possible 1,800; yesterday, even that superb record was thrown into the shade by a total score of 1,679. * * *

The speech of their captain shows that the British team have taken their ill-fortune in noble and pleasant mood. There are various theories about the cause of their failure, such as that their bullets, expanding beyond calculation in the greater heat of our climate, stuck too closely in the bore of the rifle. But a chief cause has no doubt been the superiority of our breech-loading over their muzzle-loading guns. The score of 219 out of a possible 225, made by Mr. Bruce, yesterday, not only surpasses all previous records of rifle shooting, but indicates the use of a gun in which perfection has been nearly reached. It is not at all surprising that the British team are reported as intending to supply themselves immediately with American breech-loading rifles. * * *

Messrs. Bruce, Weber, and Hyde were then addressed by Judge Stanton, and congratulated for their excellent scoring in the two days'

competition. Bruce, who made the champion score of the world, re-
plied that "SHARPS Rifle did the work, with me back of it."

—*N. Y. Daily Tribune*, Sept. 15, 1877.

The British Rifle Team.

BRIDGEPORT, CONN., Sept. 15, 1877.
Sir Henry Halford, with the members of the British team, visited
SHARPS Rifle Works to-day. Sergeant Gilder, at 1,000 yards, made
sixteen consecutive bullseyes with a new SHARPS breech-loading Rifle.

—*N. Y. Herald*, Sept. 16, 1877.

British and American Marksmen.

From the London Sporting Gazette, Sept. 29, 1877.

⁂ ⁂ ⁂ It has been suggested that the American victory is a victory
of superior rifles, not of superior marksmen, and indeed in the SHARPS
Rifle the Americans seem to have at last secured a match rifle which,
for accuracy at long ranges, is unsurpassed, perhaps unequaled. That
is a fact, however, which is not creditable to us, for the last fifteen
years our experts have been engaged in endeavoring to obtain the
best possible long-range rifle. Yet here are the Americans, with whom
long-range shooting has not been in vogue four years, producing a
rifle better, they allege, than we have been able to produce after fifteen
years' close experience. Of course it will be urged that American gun
makers have had the advantage of our experience to guide them, and
that they have in reality started from the point at which we left off.
Nevertheless, the fact still remains that the Americans, with only four
years' experience of long-range shooting, are able to beat us both in
rifles and marksmen, though we have had fifteen years' experience.
The sudden growth and rapid spread of the taste for long-range shooting in America are very remarkable, and prove that the Americans
must all along have had a latent, undeveloped aptitude for marksman-
ship, which only required to be called into existence to become uni-
versal. ⁂ ⁂ ⁂

PRICE LIST, JANUARY, 1878.

SUPERSEDING ALL PREVIOUS LISTS.

Rifles of 45 calibre having proved to give much better results and greater satisfaction to our customers, we have discontinued the manufacture of either the 44 or 50 calibre, except on special orders. The 45 calibre " Sporting " and " Business " rifles, chambered for $2\frac{1}{10}$ or $2\frac{7}{8}$ inch shells, will be found entirely effective and in every way satisfactory for either medium or heavy charges of powder. All our rifles are warranted to stand 150 grains of powder, if customers desire to use that quantity. But the *regular* charge is ample for any purpose. For long distances any powder that is not burned *in* the barrel impairs accuracy to such an extent that all benefit from the increase of force is lost, and for short or medium distances the force supplied by the regular charge is sufficient for any requirement.

Sharps Sporting Rifles.
Model 1874.

45 calibre, 30 inch octagon bbl., weight 9 to 12 lbs., open sights, polished stocks, single trigger......................$38 00
For guns exceeding 12 lbs. in weight, per lb. extra......... 1 00
Double triggers extra.................................. 4 00

Weights from 9 to 16 lbs. are kept in stock; anything heavier will have to be made to order. *As all deviation from our regular list product involves much additional outlay for hand labor, an extra charge of* TWENTY PER CENT. *will be made on such special orders, and additional time will be required to fill them.*

When orders for a given weight are received, say 12 lbs., and we have not the exact weight, we send the nearest fraction to that weight we have. The variation will not usually be more than six ounces. Special arms of any weight or length made and engraved to order.

Sharps "Business" Rifles.
Model 1874.

28 inch, round barrel, 40 and 45 cal. *Double trigger*, polished stock, weight about 10½ lbs., 40 calibre, chambered for 70 grains, and 45 calibre, 75 grains powder.....................$35 00

Can be chambered for heavier cartridges if desired, extra charge for re-chambering, each 1 00

Sharps Hunter's Rifle.
Model 1874.

Very close-shooting serviceable guns, chambered for 50 grains powder, weight about 9 lbs., 40 calibre, polished stock, open sights, single trigger, 26 inch round barrel.............$25 00

Sharps Mid Range Rifles. No. 1.
Model 1874.

Mounted with Vernier sight complete, graduated up to 600 yards, wind gauge and spirit level, also with open hunting sights, 40 calibre, 30 inch barrel, weight about 9 lbs., single trigger, 3 lbs. pull, pistol grip, checkered grip and fore-end, chambered for 70 grains powder and 330 grains lead $65 00

Sharps Mid Range No. 2.
Model 1874.

$\frac{40}{100}$ calibre, octagon 30 inch barrel, single trigger, 3 lbs. pull; weight about 9 lbs., broad hand-made butt, with checkered butt-plate, open, peep and globe sights, chambered for 50 grains powder and 265 grains lead.............................$45 00

Can be chambered for heavier cartridges, if desired. Extra charge for re-chambering................................... 1 00

Sharps Mid-Range Rifle.

Model 1878.

Mounted with Vernier sights complete, graduated up to 600 yards, wind gauge and spirit level; also with open hunting sights, 40 calibre, 30 inch barrel, weight about 9 lbs., single trigger, 3 lbs. pull, pistol grip, checkered grip and forearm, chambered for 70 grains powder, 330 grains lead. Standard style........................$75 00

In extra finish, fancy wood stock, engraving, etc., to order, up to........... 150 00

Scale of Elevations for Sharps Mid-Range Rifles.

At the shorter ranges there is less difference in elevations under varying conditions than at the long distances. The following table will be found near enough correct to find the target (with wind guage set correctly) under almost any conditions:

		One hundredths of an inch.
100	yards	0
200	"	11
300	"	24
400	"	37
500	"	51
600	"	66

Sharps Mid-Range Rifle.

Model 1878.

The Best in the World.

The following score was made with a Sharps Mid-Range Rifle, by John T. Rainey, of New Orleans, 500 yards, OFF-HAND, regulation second-class target, 70 out of a possible 75.

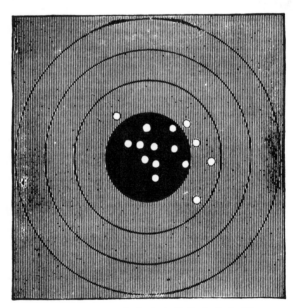

5 4 5 5 4 5 5 4 4 5 5 5 5 4—70.

Sharps New Military Rifle.

Borchardt Patent.

Sharps Carbine. Model 1878.

45 Calibre, Chambered for 70 grains Powder and 420 grains Lead.......$16.50

Sharps New Military Rifle.

Borchardt's Patent.

For safety, accuracy, penetration, range, ease of manipulation, rapidity and certainty of fire, strength, durability, and lightness of recoil, they are unequaled by any rifle made.

45 calibre, length of shell 2 1-10 inches, 75 grains powder, 420 grains lead, U. S. cartridges can be used, length of barrel 32 inches, length of rifle 48½ inches, weight without bayonet 9 pounds.

Price without bayonet................................$20 00
Price with bayonet................................... 22 50

For Governments, States, and Independent Military Organizations special prices will be given upon application. The operation of this rifle is remarkable for its simplicity and ease of manipulation. Throwing down the lever (which serves also for a trigger guard) ejects with certainty the exploded shell, and cocks the rifle; the same motion also automatically moves the safety-catch and locks the trigger, so that accidental discharge is impossible. The cartridge is now inserted and the lever returned to its position. The rifle, though now at full cock, may be carried and handled in any manner with perfect safety, there is nothing to catch in bushes, it may be pulled out of boat or wagon by the muzzle, or handled in any manner, however carelesssly (for other rifles), and it cannot be discharged, except by intentionally releasing the safety-catch and pulling the trigger.

The safety-catch is so located behind the trigger, and under the trigger-guard, that it can be instantaneously, but in no case accidentally, released.

When great rapidity of fire is desirable, as in battles, the safety-lever may be quickly removed, so that the piece can be discharged immediately upon closing the breech, and thus save one movement. The United States and Austrian are now the only great Governments who retain the obsolete outside hammer on their arms, and the question of a change is being agitated by the latter.

Objections may possibly be made to the absence of the outside hammer on account of the difficulty in executing the movement of " support arms." It should be remembered that *the manual is made for arms*, and not *arms for the manual*.

It is vastly more important, when an enemy is approaching, to be able to shoot him effectually, rather than salute him gracefully.

Sharps Long Range Rifle, Model 1878.

Used by Bruce, Selph, Weber, Blydenburgh, Allen, Jewell, Gildersleeve, Sanford, Glynn, Hawley, Arms, Eyrich, Hyde, and by nearly every other first-class shot in the country.

See diagram of targets with score; the champion score of the world made by L. C. Bruce, in the great International Match of 1877.

Champion Score of the World.

Made by Lieut. L. C. Bruce with a Sharps Long Range Rifle, in the International Match, Sept., 1877.

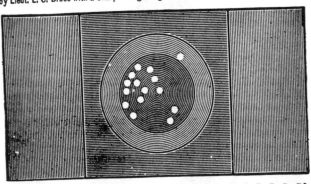

800 YARDS. Score—5 5 5 5 5 5 5 5 5 4 5 5 5 5 5—74.

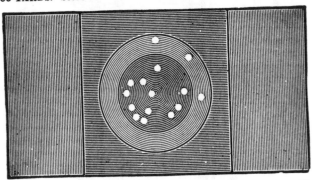

900 YARDS. Score—5 5 5 5 5 4 4 4 5 5 5 5 5 5 5—72.

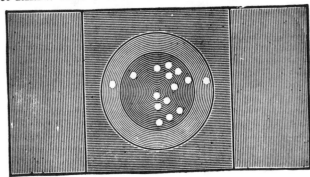

1000 YARDS. Score—5 5 5 5 4 4 5 5 5 5 5 5 5 5 5—73. Total, 219.

Sharps Long Range Rifle.
Model 1878.

Every long range rifle is fully tested by an expert up to 1,000 yards, and is guaranteed by the Company in every respect.

THE STANDARD RIFLE.—Weight just under 10 lbs., trigger 3½ lbs. pull; English walnut stock, pistol grip, checkered grip and forearm, rubber heel plate. New Vernier rear sight (optional either grip or heel), giving elevation to 1,200 yards, and measuring to one one-thousandth of an inch; wind gauge and spirit level, and one each, pin head and aperture front disk .. $100 00

Same, Vernier interchangeable to heel or grip, two bases.. 110 00

Same, with two Verniers, heel and grip complete........ 115 00

This rifle, for accuracy and strength, is the best we can make.

Same rifle to order, with extra fancy Italian stock, engraving, and extra finish.....................$125 to $300 00

The above-described long range rifles all have the new action (Borchardt's Patent). Customers desiring the outside hammer model, with common Vernier sight, will be supplied at same prices.

Elevations for Sharps Long Range Rifles.

This table is calculated for rear sight placed on grip. If it is placed on heel the elevation will be about 26 per cent. more. It is based on the average elevation from May to October. In early spring or late fall, they will be found much higher at the longer distances. On a very cold day, with a strong head wind, they may be found to be fifteen points ($\frac{15}{100}$ of an inch) higher. On a very hot moist day, with a rear wind at 800 to 1000 yards, they may be five points ($\frac{5}{100}$ of an inch) lower. It is intended that all of the new model long range rifles shall shoot same elevation; but different loading of cartridges, different holding and difference in vision in different men, may cause a variation of from three to five points. Thus it will be seen that it is only possible to make a table that is *approximately* correct.

SCALE OF ELEVATIONS.

200 yards	....	11
300 "	....	23
400 "	....	38
500 "	....	54
600 "	....	70
700 "	....	86
800 "	....	103
900 "	....	121
1000 "	....	139
1100 "	....	160
1200 "	....	180

Directions for Measuring Elevations by the Vernier Scale.

Elevations for Sharps Long Range Rifles are measured by inches, marked 1, 2, 3, etc. (On some of the old model guns the scale is marked in half inches.) These are sub-divided into twentieths of an inch, each mark on the main scale representing five one-hundredths (more commonly called points). If the bottom line of the short sliding scale be set opposite the line marked 1 on the main scale, it shows one inch elevation. To add $\frac{1}{100}$ (or one point) to this, we set the *second* line from the bottom on the *short* scale, to the line on the main scale above it. To add $\frac{2}{100}$ (or two points) we move the *third* line from the bottom on the short scale, to the line above it. To add $\frac{3}{100}$ move up the *fourth* line, and for $\frac{4}{100}$ the fifth line, then to get the $\frac{5}{100}$ the *bottom* line is now moved up to the first line above the inch mark, and we have 1 $\frac{5}{100}$ in. elevation, or, as more commonly called, one hundred and five points.

Proceed in same manner for any number of points required.

To Measure Fractions of a Point by the New Vernier.

On the lower half of the screw that moves the sliding scale will be observed grooves cut diagonally across the thread at regular intervals. Move the screw the width of one of these, and it changes the elevation one-tenth of a point, or one one-thousandth of an inch, two of them two-tenths, etc. On the centre of the screw will be observed the figures, 0, 5, 10, 15, 20, at regular intervals. From 0 to 5 changes one half a point; 0 to 10 changes one point; turning it entirely round changes two and one-half points. The new Vernier scale is an invention recently patented by the SHARPS RIFLE CO., and can be used on no other rifle. The numerous advantages it possesses over the old one will be greatly appreciated by expert riflemen. Besides the old scale measurement, it has an additional Vernier, by which any decimal of a point $\frac{1}{10}$ (one-thousandth of an inch), $\frac{2}{10}$, $\frac{3}{10}$, etc. can be moved in elevation with accuracy. The slender screw, which gave so much trouble when bent, is done away with, and the rifleman can be certain when he fixes his elevation at any point that it will not be found at some other point after the peep cup be tightened.

General Directions for Use and Care of Sharps Long Range Rifles.

A fine long range rifle is a somewhat expensive toy, but one of our manufacture will last a life time, if properly cared for. After use, it should be thoroughly cleaned, *inside and outside*. It should then be thoroughly oiled *inside and outside*, then the oil should be thoroughly rubbed off *inside and outside*. Use only fine gun or sperm oil. With these precautions, no trouble will be had from rust. The breech-block (or slide) will seldom require taking out for cleaning if bearings are kept well oiled. When necessary to take out, refer to directions on page 38. The forearm of the long range gun must first be removed, after which directions apply. The parts contained in the breech-block should be oiled occasionally.

Ammunition—Reloading Shells, etc., etc.

The cartridges furnished by the SHARPS RIFLE Co. are made with the utmost care, and can be depended upon for any kind of shooting, but the rifleman who uses many, will find it a measure of economy to re-load his shells. This can be done a great number of times, especially those fired in the long range gun, in which the chambering is so close and the breech action so solid that there is scarcely any strain upon the shell. A wad-cutter, bullet-seater, shell-crimper, and loading-tube are the principal tools required. The shell should be thoroughly cleaned, and the easiest and most effective way to do this (we refer now to long range shells) is to have a little hand-brush and a bottle of water on the field with your " Kit." A quarter of a minute's rubbing with the wet brush, inside and out, effectually cleans it, and nothing remains, when you wish to reload, but to recap it when dry (THE PRIMER OR CAP SHOULD ALWAYS BE SEATED WELL HOME BEFORE LOADING). If the cleaning is delayed till the foul becomes dry and hard, then the shells may be soaked in vinegar for five minutes and afterward thoroughly washed in hot water. In all cases they must be thoroughly dry before recapping and reloading. When cleaned at home, it is better to remove the exploded cap before cleaning the shell. To do this, bore a hole in a piece of hard wood, the size of the body of the shell, which will leave its rim even with the surface, place the shell therein, take a cap awl and, with a slight tap with a hammer or mallet, perforate the exploded cap a little one side of the centre, so as not to strike the anvil, and pry it out; clean out the débris, if any, around the anvil. The shell being cleaned and dry, if you find the bullet fits loosely, reduce the mouth of the shell with the crimper, put a new cap in place, being careful to seat it below the base of the shell so it will not be touched by the closing breech-block. This can be done by placing it again in the wooden block and tapping it smartly home with a mallet. The long-range cartridges made at the factory are charged with one hundred grains powder. To get this quantity into the shell it is necessary to use a loading-tube. This is made of brass, about 30 inches long, one end made large enough to just take in and hold the small end of the shell, and the other end made funnel-shaped. Place the shell in position and pour the powder *slowly* enough, to have it pack at least $\frac{1}{16}$ of an inch from the mouth of the shell. Over it put a thin wad of draughting paper and place the bullet within the shell with the fingers, making sure you do not tear the paper patch. Now place the ball seater over it and press the ball gently down to the powder, and the cartridge is complete. Two things that are of *vital* importance to be observed are : *First.* that every shell should be filled with powder to exactly the same height. If the pouring through the tube does not carry it to the right point, a gentle tapping on the sides of the shells with another shell may do it; if not, reject that shell. Different batches of powder of same brand often vary, so that it is found impossible to get in one hundred grains; in such a case use one to three grains less, as may be found necessary, taking care not to crush the powder. The *second vital point* is to see that the paper patch does not get torn while seating bullet in shell, and when inserting the cartridge in the rifle be careful and not catch the patch on the rifling. Observe before inserting that the bullet has not gotten loose in the shell. If it has moved away from the powder it will fall short of the mark.

Our estimate of quantity of powder is based on the best " F. G." brands in general use. A stronger powder can be used in our rifles with perfect safety, but is liable to be destructive to cartridge shells, and, we think, gives no better results. Expert riflemen, however, differ so greatly on this point, that we prefer to leave our customers to decide it from personal experience. We have found the powder of the Laflin & Rand Powder Co. and the Oriental Powder Co. all that could be desired.

To get the best results from a long range gun, it is important that it should be thoroughly cleaned after each shot. There are many methods of doing this among riflemen. The following will be found speedy and satisfactory. First loosen the foul with a slightly wet brush passed through the barrel (*always perform all cleaning operations from the breech*), then pass a tight-fitting cork through. Follow this with a flannel rag cut to proper size, on a rod with button end. By this process two or three rags will serve for a days' shooting. Glover & Budd, whose advertisement will be found on another page, manufacture a felt cleaner which will be found very effectual. Some riflemen oil the barrel after cleaning. There is no objection to this if it is only done uniformly. In fact, uniformity of treatment of the barrel from shot to shot is of more importance than anything else in producing uniform results. Therefore, make uniformity your maxim! Uniform loading of cartridge, uniform treatment of rifle and uniform holding will give uniform shooting!

Always keep a minute record of your shooting, whether practice or matches, giving distance shot over, elevation and wind gauge used, direction of wind, your estimate of its strength, temperature, state of atmosphere, moist or dry, etc., etc. This will in time become an invaluable record, and will enable you generally to " find " the target the first shot.

For weighing powder charges for rifles, Apothecaries' scales and the Apothecaries' table of weights and measures are used. The table is :

20 grains, 1 scruple.	3 scruples, 1 drachm.
8 drachms, 1 oz.	12 ounces, 1 lb.

Powder, however, is bought and sold by Avoirdupois weight, which has 16 ounces to the pound. The grain weight is the same in all tables. The pound Avoirdupois contains 7,000 grains.

1 lb. powder will load 140   50 gr. cartridges.
1 "   "   "   "   93 75 "   "
1 "   "   "   "   70 100 "   "

A Drachm Avoirdupois is equal to $27\frac{11}{32}$ grains.

Wind Gauge and Spirit Level................ $10.00

Globe Sight.. $1.00.

Knife Blade Sight,
German silver.... 70c.

Base for Vernier on grip $2.00

New Patent Vernier, $10.
Measures to $\frac{1}{1000}$ of an
inch.

Base for Vernier on heel (adjustable laterally).... $3.00

Open Front Sight. . . . . 50c.

Wind Gauge (front view).

Mid-Range Vernier
Scale . . . . $8.00.   Peep Sight (Sporting). $4.00

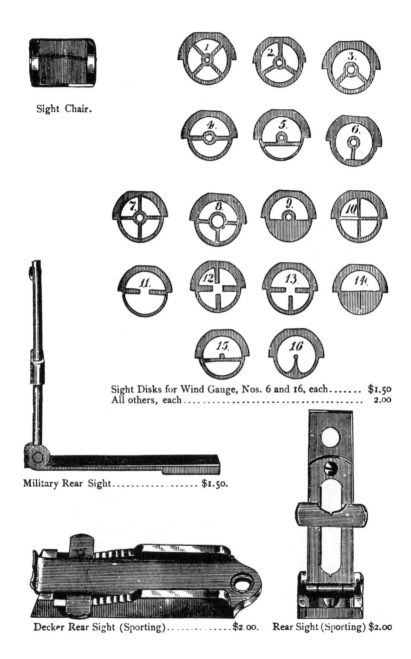

Sight Chair.

Sight Disks for Wind Gauge, Nos. 6 and 16, each....... $1.50
All others, each.................................... 2.00

Military Rear Sight................ .... $1.50.

Decker Rear Sight (Sporting).............$2.00.   Rear Sight (Sporting) $2.00

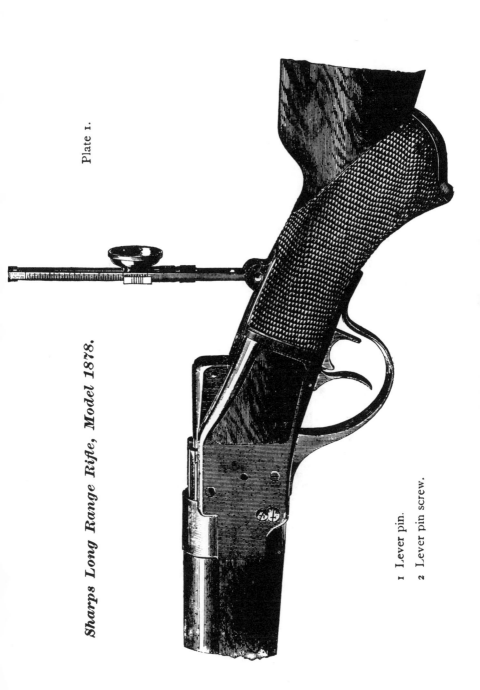

Sharps Long Range Rifle, Model 1878.

Plate 1.

1 Lever pin.
2 Lever pin screw.

Sharps Rifle, Model 1878.

Sectional view, showing action at moment of discharge.

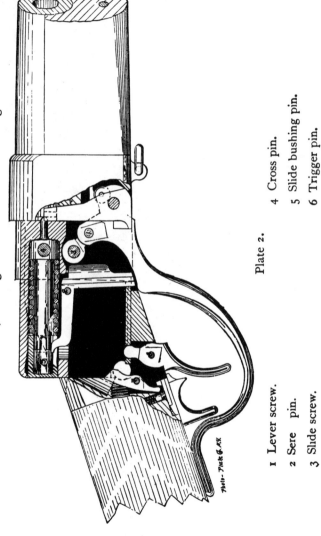

Plate 2.

1 Lever screw.
2 Sere pin.
3 Slide screw.
4 Cross pin.
5 Slide bushing pin.
6 Trigger pin.
7 Safety lever pin.

Sharps Rifle, Model 1878.
Sectional View, Showing Action Closed.

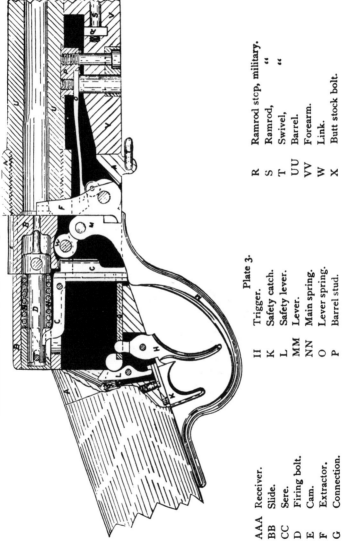

Plate 3.

AAA	Receiver.
BB	Slide.
CC	Sere.
D	Firing bolt.
E	Cam.
F	Extractor.
G	Connection.
II	Trigger.
K	Safety catch.
L	Safety lever.
MM	Lever.
NN	Main spring.
O	Lever spring.
P	Barrel stud.
R	Ramrod stop, military.
S	Ramrod, "
T	Swivel, "
UU	Barrel.
VV	Forearm.
W	Link.
X	Butt stock bolt.

Sharps Rifle, Model 1878.

Sectional view, showing action open to receive cartridge.

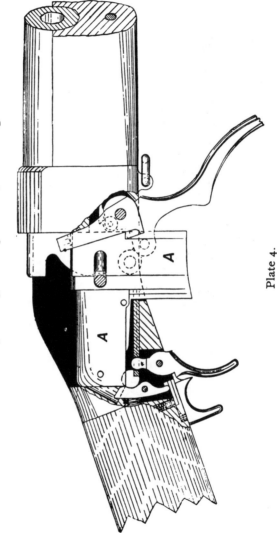

Plate 4.

AA Slide or breech block.

Model 1878.

To Take the Breech Mechanism Apart.

Loosen the rear screw under the barrel. This will relieve the pressure of the lever spring.

Cock the gun by opening and closing.

Bring down the lever (MM, plate 3) half way.

Take out lever-pin (1, plate 1) on which the lever rotates. This pin is held in place by the small screw (2, plate 1) directly above it. Turn this screw to the left until the circular cut in its side is on a line with the lever-pin, and the latter can then be removed.

Pull lever out of the joint.

Replace lever-pin so as to hold extractor in place.

Remove screw (1, plate 2) which connects lever and link, through hole in the left side of slide.

Take out lever. Push slide (AA, plate 4) up and out, and then take out extractor (F, plate 3).

Stripping Slide.

Uncock slide and push out sere-pin (2, plate 2) and remove sere (CC, plate 3). Take out pin at rear end of slide (5, plate 2).

Take out slide plug and main spring (NN, plate 3).

Drive cross-pin (4, plate 2) out of firing bolt, and remove same.

Remove link (W, plate 3) by taking last screw out of slide.

To Remove Trigger, Safety, and Safety Lever.

Drive out trigger-pin (6, plate 2) and safety pin above it (7, plate 2).

Pull back safety catch (K, plate 3) and pull out trigger.

Push forward safety catch as far as it will go, and it will drop out, together with the safety lever above it.

To Take off Butt Stock.

Remove butt-plate and unscrew, with long screw driver, the bolt which fastens stock to the frame.

Reassembling Breech.

Put on butt-stock. Replace safety-catch, safety-lever, and trigger. Assemble slide and cock it. Push safety-catch into notch of trigger. Put in extractor and lever-pin.

Insert slide and push it down, keeping extractor close to its place, in base of barrel. Attach lever.

Take out lever-pin, bring lever into the joint, replace the pin, and secure it by giving small screw above it half a turn to the right.

Tighten the screw which was loosened under the barrel.

Never use a hammer or other force in either stripping or assembling this system. If the parts are in proper position, everything will go into place easily.

To detach the lever, breech-block, and extractor of model 1874, throw down the lever, depress the small spur contiguous to the arm of the lever key in the right side of the receiver, and swing the arm of the lever key a half turn, withdrawing it, and the parts are released. To replace them, put the parts in the same relative position as they occupied when the lever key was being removed, and they will readily move to place and be secured by the lever key.

———

Reloading Implements, Sights, etc., etc.

Bullet Mould—" Sporting," " Business," " Hunting," and
   " Mid-Range " $3.00
Wad Cutter.. .75
Cap Awl.. .25
Lubricator Mould.................................. .50
Bullet Seater..................................... 1.00
Follower (for Seating Wads)........................ .50
Charger.. .25
                          —— $6.25

LONG RANGE RELOADING IMPLEMENTS.

Swage }
Slug Mould } $10.00
Cap, or Primer Awl............................... .25
Bullet Seater.................................... 1.00
Wad Cutter...................................... .75
Charger... .25
Brass Loading Tube, 45 cal., 34 inches............ 3.00
Shell Crimper for Long-Range Shells.............. 3.00
                          —— 18.25

Charges for measuring, 50, 60, 70, 75, 77, 90, 95, 100, 105,
   110, or 120 grains of powder, each.................... .25
Shell Reducing Punch and Die—for reducing Shells expanded
   in firing... 6.00
Bullet Swages with Slug Mould, Long or Mid Range..... 10.00
Globe Sights, interchangeable with open Sights............ 1.00
Peep Sights (Sporting)............................... 4.00
    "   price for graduating, each.................... .50
Beach Combination Front Sights....................... 3.00
Telescope Sights...................................... 35.00
Interchangeable Pin Ball or Aperture Disks for Wind Gauge,
   each 1.50
Interchangeable Wind Gauge Disks, other styles, to order only, 2.00
Double Triggers, extra................................ 4.00

Crescent Butt Plates (nickel or silver-plated), extra.......... $5.00
Cleaning Rods.. .25
    "   extra long, varnished, with handles.......... .50
Cleaning Brushes, with rods............................. .50
Jewell's Score Books, with flexible morocco covers, net...... .50
Russet Leather Slings................................. 1.50
Sling Swivel, 50c.; fitting same, 50c.................... 1.00
Sharps Powder, per lb................................ .50
Lubricating Disks, per 1000....... .... 1.25
    "   Material, per lb........................... 1.00
Primers, per 1000.................................... 3.00
Wads, per 1000...................................... .50
Cut Paper Patches, per 1000........................... .50
Patch Paper, per 100 sheets........................... 2.00
Corks used in loading shells, when a charge of powder less
    than the capacity of the shell is required, per 100........ .25

Glover & Budd's Patent Cleaning Implements.

Very highly recommended.

Fixture for Rod..................................... $0.10
Swabs with Bolt, Nuts, and Washers, complete, each......... .25
Felt Swabs (for renewals), per doz...................... 1.50
Paravaseline Lubricator, per box........................ .25
Rouge Paste, per box................................. .25

Cases for Rifles.

Canvas, Gun Shaped.................................. $2.50
Stiff Leather, Gun Shaped............................. 7.00
Bridle Leather, Gun Shaped, with Shoulder Strap........... 10.00
Hard Leather, Trunk Shaped........................... 20.00

Monograms, animals, and other designs elegantly engraved on our
arms, the price for which is governed by the time occupied in its exe-
cution. Customers can order engraving to the amount of $5, $10,
$15, $20, or more, as desired. Engraving can be done only on new
work, and before the parts are case-hardened.

Component Parts, Model 1874.

Barrels for Sharps Rifles, weighing when assembled:

9 to 12 lbs. 30 inch	....	$10.00
12 to 13 " "	....	11.00
13 to 14 " "	....	12.00
14 to 15 " "	....	13.00
15 to 16 " "	....	14.00

Mid-Range Barrels	$15.00
Adjusting, testing, and warranty....................	10.00—25.00
Long-Range Barrels.............................	20.00
Adjusting, testing, and warranty....................	30.00—50.00
Barrel Stud....................................	.25
Bridle	.50
Butt Plate....................................	1.00
" Rubber..................................	2.00
Bands, each....................................	.50
Band Springs..................................	.20
Butt Stock, M'ch'd..............................	3.00
" Broad	4.00
" Pistol Grip...........................	10.00
" Extra for Fancy American Walnut............	5.00
" " Italian Walnut.....................	10.00
Checking Butt Stock and Forearm...................	5.00
Extractor	.50
Escutcheon	.10
Firing Bolt....................................	1.00
Guard Strap, Single Trigger......................	1.00
" Double Trigger........................	1.75
Hammer	1.50
Lever	1.75
" Spring....................................	.50
" Key	.50
Lock Plate....................................	1.25
Main Spring....................................	1.00
Nose Cap (Military).............................	.50
Receiver......................................	7.00

Spirit Level			$3.00
Slide			2.00
Sight, Front (Sporting)			.50
" " Knife-blade (German Silver)			.70
" Rear, complete			2.00
" Peep			4.00
" Globe			1.00
Stirrup			.20
Sere			.50
Swivel			.50
" Bar and Ring			.50
Screws, ½ inch, and under			.05
" over ½ inch			.10
Toggle			.40
Triggers			.50
" Double, complete			4.00
Tumbler			1.00
" Fly			.25
Tip Stock			2.00
Vernier Leaf			4.00
" Slide			1.25
" Cup			1.50
" Base			3.00
" Studs, 2			.75
" Spring			.50
" Adjusting Screw			.60
" Check Nuts, 2			.40
" Base Screw			.40
Vernier Sights, Complete, Mid Range			8.00
" " Long Range, Patent			10.00
" " " Extra Long			12.00
Wind Gauge and Spirit Level, complete			10.00
" Slide			3.50
" Base			1.25
" Stud			.60
" Screw			.75
" Nuts, 2			.40
" Disks, 2			3.00
" Spring Button			.25
" " Rivet			.15
" " Pin			.15

Component Parts, Model 1878.

1	Receiver	$7.00
2	Slide	2.50
3	Lever	1.75
4	Main Spring	.25
5	Firing Bolt	.50
6	Sere	.75
7	Safety	.60
8	Lever Spring	.50
9	Extractor	.60
10	Trigger	.50
11	Safety Lever	.30
12	Barrel Stud	.25
13	Swivel	.10
14	Butt Stock Bolt	.50
15	Slide Bushing	.30
16	Cams	.75
17	Connection	.50
18	Link	.30
19	Rear Band	.50
20	Front Band	.50
21	Tip	.50
22	Ramrod Stop	.15
23	Butt Plate	1.00
24	Escutcheon	.50
25	Safety Catch Spring	.10
26	Sere Spring	.10
27	Forearm Screw	.10
28	Lever Spring Screw	.10
29	Lever Joint Pin	.10
30	Rear Band Screw	.10
31	Sere Spring Pin	.05
32	Slide Screw	.05
33	Safety Spring Pin	.05
34	Lever-roll Pin	.05
35	Swivel Pin	.05
36	Cam Pin	.05
37	Lever Roll	.10
38	Front Band Screw	.10
39	Lever Joint Pin Screw	.05
40	Cam Screw	.05
41	Tip Screw	.05
42	Safety Lever Pin	.10
43	Block Screw	.05
44	Trigger Pin	.10
45	Firing Bolt Pin	.10
46	Butt Plate Screw	.10
47	Lever Screw	.10
48	Sere Pin and Slide	.10
49	Bushing Pin	.10
50	Ramrod (Steel)	.50

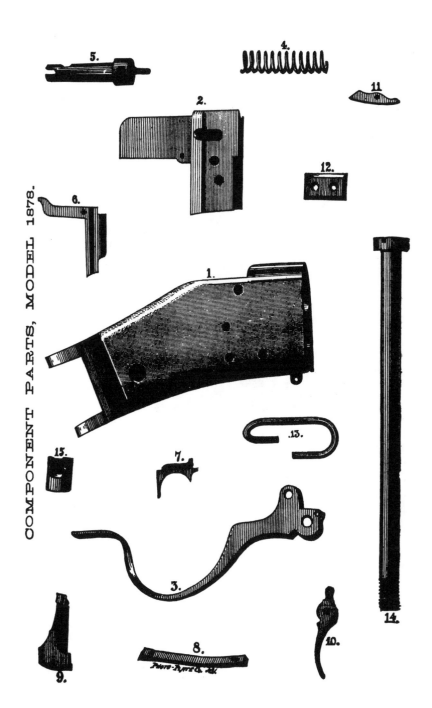

COMPONENT PARTS, MODEL 1878.

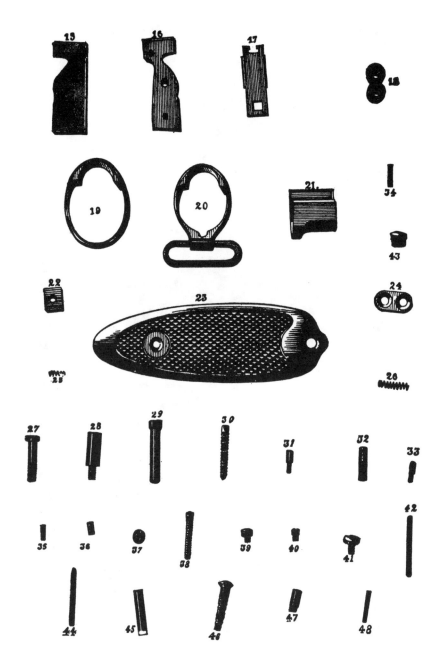

Cartridges, Bullets, Shells, &c.

The following show exact size of Cartridges.

When loading, if the Cartridge does not enter the chamber of barrel by the pressure of the thumb, do not attempt to pry it in. It is dangerous.

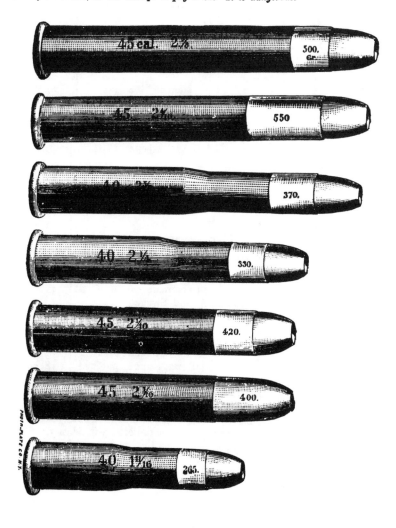

Cartridges.

Calibre.	Length of Shell.	Weight of Powder.	Length of Bullet.	Weight of Bullet.	Price per 1000.
	Inches.	Grains.	Inches.	Grains.	
40/100	1 11/16	50	1 5/16 Patched.	265	$37 00
40/100	2 1/2	70	1 1/8 "	330	39 25
40/100	2 5/8	90	1 1/4 "	370	47 75
44/100	2 1/4	75	7/8 Naked.	297	39 25
44/100	2 1/4	75	1 1/8 Patched.	405	41 25
44/100	2 5/8	90	1 3/8 "	500	53 00
44/100	2 5/8	105	1 13/32 "	520	55 00
45/100	2 1/10	70	1 1/10 Naked.	400	40 25
45/100	2 1/10	70	1 1/10 Patched.	420	41 25
45/100	2 1/10	100	1 13/32 "	550	55 00
45/100	2 7/8	100	1 1/2 "	500	54 00
50/100	1 3/4	70	1 Naked.	425	39 75
50/100	2 1/2	100	1 1/10 Patched.	473	53 00

Bullets.

Cal.	Length of Bullet.	Weight of Bullet.	Kind of Bullet.	Price per 1,000.
	Inches.	Grains.		
40/100	3/4	238	Naked (2 cannelures).........	$8.75
40/100	1 5/16	265	Patched and Swaged.........	9.25
40/100	1 1/8	330	" "	10.25
40/100	1 1/4	370	" "	11.50
44/100	7/8	297	Naked (2 cannelures).........	10.25
44/100	1 1/8	405	Patched and Swaged.........	12.50
44/100	1 3/8	500	" "	13.00
44/100	1 13/32	520	" "	14.50
45/100	1 1/10	400	Naked (2 cannelures).........	11.75
45/100	1 1/10	420	Patched and Swaged.........	13.00
45/100	1 3/8	500	" "	13.25
45/100	1 13/32	550	" "	15.00
50/100	1	425	Naked (3 cannelures).........	12.25
50/100	1 1/10	473	Patched and Swaged.........	13.50
45/100	1 11/16	550	Special Long Range, patched.	18.00

The bullets comprised in the above list are made with the greatest care, the lead being alloyed to a proper degree to insure accuracy and prevent leading the rifle barrel. The patched bullets are swaged under powerful presses, which secures the greatest uniformity in density. The patches are cut of bank note paper of even thickness, manufactured for this Company expressly for the purpose, and are put on with the utmost exactness. The special long-range bullet composed of an alloy known only to and exclusively manufactured by this Company, is giving very fine results.

Brass, Centre Fire, Reloading Shells.

$\frac{40}{100}$ calibre,	$1\frac{11}{16}$ inches long,	per 1000	....	$17.50
$\frac{40}{100}$ "	$2\frac{1}{4}$ "	"	....	19.00
$\frac{40}{100}$ "	$2\frac{5}{8}$ "	"	....	25.50
$\frac{44}{100}$ "	$2\frac{1}{4}$ "	"	....	21.25
$\frac{44}{100}$ "	$2\frac{5}{8}$ "	"	....	25.50
$\frac{45}{100}$ "	$2\frac{1}{10}$ "	"	....	19.00
$\frac{45}{100}$ "	$2\frac{4}{10}$ "	"	....	23.25
$\frac{45}{100}$ "	$2\frac{7}{8}$ "	"	....	25.50
$\frac{50}{100}$ "	$1\frac{3}{4}$ "	"	....	17.50
$\frac{50}{100}$ "	$2\frac{5}{8}$ "	"	....	23.25

To Reload Shells for Sporting Rifles.

[See directions on page 28, for cleaning Shells.]

It is unnecessary to weigh the powder for these cartridges. If the shells be enlarged so that the bullet fits loosely, they should be reduced with the shell reducer, which can be procured at the armory or of any of the agents of the Company.

Charge with the desired quantity of powder, placing a pasteboard wad upon the powder, and force it down the full length of the follower. Insert upon the wad a lubricant disk composed of one part pure beeswax to two parts sperm oil in weight, to occupy three-sixteenths of an inch in length in the shell.

Dip the base of naked bullets up to the forward ring in melted lubricating compound, taking care to fill the groover

Place the bullet in the chamber of the bullet seater, introduce the shell, and press it home with the hand.

Wipe the cartridge clean, and it is ready for use.

In casting bullets, heat the moulds nearly as hot as the molten lead, having first cleaned them of all oil.

Every gun case contains sufficient room to pack reloading implements and a quantity of ammunition, and the cost of transportation will be but slightly increased by such an addition. Ammunition procured from the Armory is certain to be entirely reliable, and at a reasonable cost. No owner of a Sharps Rifle can afford to be without a set of re-loading implements manufactured by the Company, which are *the very best made*. By reloading cartridge shells, two-thirds of the cost of ammunition may be saved.

Patent Number:	Date:	Description:
5763	Sept. 12, 1848	Basic patent vertically sliding breech
6960	Dec. 18, 1849	Method of revolving pistol hammer
9308	Oct. 5, 1852	Basic patent, pellet primer
16072	Nov. 11, 1856	Revolving breech pin and breech bush
22752	Jan. 25, 1859	Longitudinally sliding breech
22753	Jan. 25, 1859	Revolving selective firing pin-pistols
30765	Nov. 27, 1860	Revolving block for pistols
32790	July 6, 1861	Breech-loading improvement
32899	July 23, 1861	Notched quadrant-type rear sight
33546	Oct. 22, 1861	For metallic cartridge
33607	Oct. 29, 1861	For metallic cartridge
37057	Dec. 2, 1862	Rifling machine
62077	Feb. 12, 1867	For metallic cartridge
118752	Sept. 5, 1871	For metallic cartridge
137625	April 8, 1873	For metallic cartridge
Reissue 1199	Jan. 18, 1861	Reissue Jan. 25, 1859 patent
Reissue 2480	Feb. 12, 1867	Reissue Jan. 25, 1859 patent
Reissue 2481	Feb. 12, 1867	Reissue Jan. 25, 1859 patent

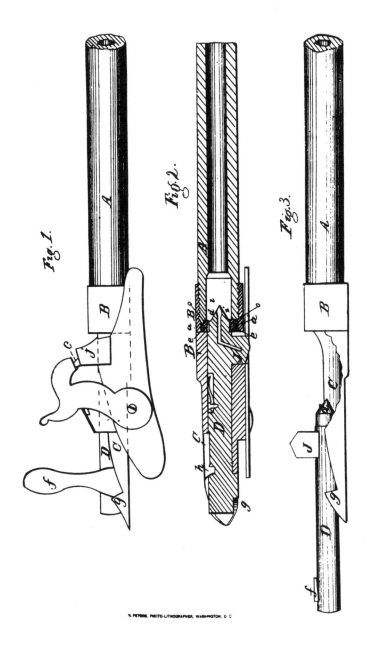

Fig. 1.

Fig. 2.

Fig. 3.

UNITED STATES PATENT OFFICE.

C. SHARPS, OF PHILADELPHIA, PENNSYLVANIA.

IMPROVEMENT IN BREECH-LOADING GUNS.

Specification forming part of Letters Patent No. **16,072**, dated November 11, 1856.

To all whom it may concern:

Be it known that I, CHRISTIAN SHARPS, of the city and county of Philadelphia, and State of Pennsylvania, have invented certain new and useful Improvements in Breech-Loading Fire-Arms; and I do hereby declare that the following is a full, clear, and exact description of my said invention, reference being had to the accompanying drawings, in which—

Figure 1 represents a side elevation of certain portions of a breech-loading rifle constructed according to the principles of my invention. Fig. 2 represents a longitudinal vertical section of the same, and Fig. 3 represents a side elevation of certain portions of the rifle with the breech-pin withdrawn for loading.

My invention relates to that class of fire-arms which are loaded at the breech, or in which the butt of the barrel may be opened to permit the insertion of the charge.

The object of my invention is to render the firing of the charge from the primer more certain. I have also combined and arranged the parts in such manner that the part of the breech which is most affected by use may be readily renewed, and that the joint does not permit the escape of smoke and gas.

My improved fire-arm is constructed in such manner that it unites the advantages of cheapness in manufacture, facility in operation, and great simplicity, while at the same time the parts are combined and arranged in such manner that the cartridge is pierced and the powder is worked into the channel leading to the primer by the operation of locking the sliding breech-pin in the place it occupies at the time the charge is fired. The fire-arm is also constructed in such manner that the sliding breech-pin may be readily removed when the barrel is to be cleaned, and again replaced without requiring the employment of tools.

In the accompanying drawings, the barrel A of the fire-arm is screwed at its butt into a breech, B, which is situated at the front end of a slide, C, in which a sliding breech-pin, D, is constructed to slide to and fro. The breech is open at its hinder end, where a shoulder, *e*, is formed to retain a removable bush, *o*, which forms the hinder extremity of the chamber in which the cartridge is inserted. The bush *o* is cylindrical, its interior bore being of suf-

ficient diameter to permit the easy insertion of the cartridge. Its exterior fits easily in the breech, and it has a collar, *i*, at its front end corresponding with the shoulder *e* in the breech, so that it cannot pass through the latter. The interior bore of the bush has a series of ring-grooves formed in it to receive tallow or other similar substance, by which the breech-pin is lubricated, and a ring-washer, *a*, of leather or other similar substance, is inserted between the collar upon the bush and the shoulder in the breech, to pack the joint and prevent the escape of smoke and gas.

As has before been said, the bush fits easily in the breech. It is inserted in its place before the barrel is screwed into the breech, and may be readily removed when the barrel has been unscrewed by simply driving it forward. The cylindrical opening in the bush is closed by the sliding breech-pin. This latter consists of a cylindrical piece of metal, which slides freely in the semi-cylindrical slide C that projects backward from the breech. It is turned off smaller at its front end to fit into the bore of the bush, and it terminates in a conical spoon-piercer, *d*, by which the butt of the cartridge is opened to permit the entrance of the fire from the primer. The breech-pin is fitted with the tube *c*, upon which the primer is exploded by the cock of the lock, and it is perforated to permit the fire to pass forward into the cartridge. The hinder end of the breech-pin is furnished with a handle, *f*, by which the breech-pin is manipulated, and which, when the gun is ready for firing, stands erect, as shown at Fig. 1. The lower end of this handle forms a latch which, engaging against a shoulder, *g*, formed upon the slide C, prevents the movement of the breech-pin during the firing of the charge. The breech-pin may be turned in the slide a quarter of a revolution from right to left, to permit it to be disengaged from the shoulder *g*, and the slide C is of sufficient length to enable the breech-pin to be slid backward a sufficient distance to permit a cartridge to be laid in the slide between the front end of the breech-pin and the breech of the gun.

On the side of the slide opposite to the handle of the breech-pin a stump, *h*, is formed, against which the base *j* of the tube *c* abuts when the breech-pin is drawn back to limit

122

e movement of the breech-pin when it is rawn backward. The part of the slide opposite to this stump is low enough to permit e base *j* of the tube to be moved past the ump *h* by turning the breech-pin from left right when the breech-pin is drawn back, that the breech-pin may be withdrawn from e slide; but the portion of this side of the ide which extends between the depression pposite the stump *h* and the depression or cket in the lock-plate in which the base of e tube is received when the breech-pin is in e position for firing is made high enough to revent the turning of the breech-pin into the osition in which it may be withdrawn from e slide until the base *j* of the tube is in con ct with the stump *h*. By this arrangement e accidental dropping of the sliding breech-in is avoided, as it can only be removed from e slide when it occupies one position in re ect to it, and when it is in this position a ositive movement is required to disengage it om the stump. The construction of the arts is in fact analogous to the method in hich a bayonet is combined with the muzzle f a fire-arm, and the combination possesses e great advantage of simplicity, while at the me time it permits the easy removal of the reech-pin to enable the fire-arm to be cleaned, nd dispenses with the use of screws or other milar devices so generally used to secure the pparatus which closes the breech in breech-ading fire-arms.

In order that the parts may not become ogged with dirt, they are fitted together with great deal of play, and to prevent the breech-in from being jarred out of its place a spring, , is sunk in a recess in it to bear against the ide, and thus create sufficient friction to pre ent the movement of the breech-pin without e application of force. The bush *o*, which rms the hinder extremity of the chamber in hich the charge is received, may be readily moved when injured by use, and may be re laced by a new one by simply unscrewing e barrel of the fire-arm. The elastic washer packs the joint tightly and prevents the es pe of smoke, thus rendering a more rigid echanical attachment of the bush to the reech unnecessary, and putting it in the ower of the most ordinary soldier to repair is fire-arm when breech-burnt.

When the fire-arm is not in use, the several arts above described occupy the positions in hich they are shown in Figs. 1 and 2. In rder to load, the cock of the lock is raised. he handle *f* is then turned from right to left

to a horizontal position. This movement disengages the breech-pin in the slide, so that it may be drawn backward by means of the handle until the base *j* of the tube comes in contact with the stump *h* of the slide. A cartridge is now laid in the slide in front of the breech-pin, and the operator, again applying his hand to the handle *f*, moves the breech-pin forward and forces the cartridge into the breech. When the bullet at the front end of the cartridge strikes the shoulder at the front end of the chamber, the farther forward movement of the cartridge is prevented, and as the breech-pin is still shoved forward to close the breech its conical spoon pierces the butt of the cartridge, so that the powder in the latter is worked into the perforation leading to the tube as the breech-pin is turned to bring the tube into the proper position for the explosion of the primer. The lock of the fire-arm I have represented in the accompanying drawings is fitted with my patent primer. The invention I have described is, however, equally adapted for the employment of Maynard's primer or for the ordinary percussion cap.

The invention I have described is susceptible of modification and alteration without affecting the principle embodied in it; hence it may with great advantage be applied to fire-arms already constructed.

I am aware that the breech of a fire-arm has heretofore been closed by a plug breech-pin connected therewith by a bayonet attachment, and that beveled or spoon-formed piercers have been used to pierce cartridges. I am also aware that a bush has been used in that part of the breech which is liable to burn by continued use. I therefore lay no claim to the invention of such devices of themselves; but

What I claim as my invention, and desire to secure by Letters Patent, is—

1. The combination and arrangement of a spoon-formed cartridge-piercer with the turning breech-pin of a breech-loading fire-arm, whereby the powder is more effectually worked into the channel leading to the primer by the operation of locking the breech-pin in its place.

2. The combination of a removable bush and elastic packing-ring with the breech of a fire-arm, substantially as herein set forth.

In testimony whereof I have hereunto subscribed my name.

CHRISTIAN SHARPS.

Witnesses:
E. A. HAWKINS,
WILLIAM HAWKINS.

C. SHARPS.
Revolver.

No. 6,960.

Patented Dec. 18, 1849.

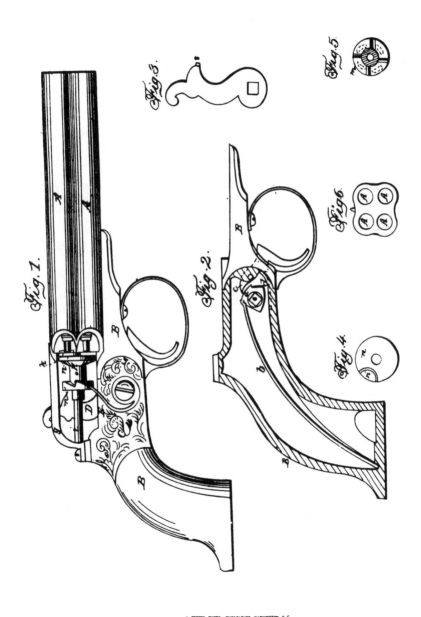

UNITED STATES PATENT OFFICE.

CHRISTIAN SHARPS, OF WASHINGTON, DISTRICT OF COLUMBIA.

IMPROVED METHOD OF REVOLVING THE HAMMERS OF REPEATING FIRE-ARMS.

Specification forming part of Letters Patent No. **6,960**, dated December 1?, 1849.

To all whom it may concern:

Be it known that I, CHRISTIAN SHARPS, of Washington, in the District of Columbia, have invented a new and useful Improvement in Repeating Fire-Arms with Stationary Barrels and a Revolving Cock; and I do hereby declare that the following is a full, clear, and exact description of my improvement, reference being had to the accompanying drawings, which form part of this specification, and in which—

Figure 1 represents a side view of a four-barreled repeating-pistol with my improvement adapted thereto. Fig. 2 is a view of the handle of the same with the side removed to show the construction of the lock. Fig. 3 is an elevation of the cocking-lever; Fig. 4, a face view of the hammer; Fig. 5, a back view of the double ratchet on the hammer, and Fig. 6 is an end view of the muzzle of the pistol.

My invention consists in attaching to a revolving hammer a double-faced ratchet which is acted upon by two levers, which together turn the hammer the angular distance required to discharge the barrels consecutively.

In the drawings, A A A A are four pistol-barrels, connected together and secured to a stock or handle, B, which contains within it the tumbler a, the mainspring b, and the sear c, with its spring d. The tumbler is secured to a short shaft, e, whose extremities, passing transversely through a lock-plate, C, on each side of the stock, are squared to receive two levers, D E. The tumbler is acted upon by the mainspring b, whose heel rests in a step formed in the lower part of the handle, and it is arranged to act endwise upon the tumbler. The periphery of the latter is notched to catch against the sear c, which in this instance is the prolongation of the trigger. The hammer H is in this instance formed of two disks, m and n, attached to a sleeve, o, and slides upon a spindle, i, whose front extremity is secured to the breech of the barrels, its hinder extremity being supported by a hammer-guard, g, which protects the hammer and at the same time serves to lengthen the line of sight. The front disk, n, has a projection, n', upon its face to strike the caps placed on the nipples screwed into the breech of the barrels. The hinder disk, m, has a ratchet upon each of its

faces, which are acted upon respectively by the two levers D E, fitted to the squared extremities of the tumbler-shaft. One of these levers, D, has a snug, s, Fig. 3, projected from its face, which acts upon the ratches on the hinder face of the disk m. It also serves to bend the spring and to transmit its tensive force to the sliding hammer. The other lever, E, has a hooked extremity to act upon the ratchet-teeth on the front face of the disk m, and is formed of a spring, which, bearing against the front face of the disk, forces the hammer to follow the cocking-lever D when the latter is drawn back in cocking the pistol. The ratchet-teeth on each face of the disk m correspond in number with the number of barrels; but those of the back face are situated between those on the front, as shown in dotted lines in Fig. 5. In cocking the pistol the hammer slides backward in a straight line upon its spindle, while the levers D and E describe an arc of a circle whose center is the axis of the tumbler-shaft. As this arc deviates downward from the straight line described by the hammer the hooked extremity of the spring-lever E, acting upon the ratch in contact with it, draws it downward and turns the hammer half the angular distance between two consecutive nipples. When the tumbler is released from the sear by the tripping of the trigger by the finger the cocking-lever D, being forced forward by the mainspring, drives the hammer before it, and at the same time its snug, acting against the ratch in contact with it, shoves that side of the hammer upward, and thus turns it the remaining half of the distance required to bring it directly opposite the nipple. Thus by successive cockings and trippings of the trigger the same hammer is made to discharge each barrel in turn.

It will be perceived that as the hammer is turned half the required distance in its retrograde movement and the remaining half in its direct movement the angular distance between two adjoining barrels may be made much larger than it can when the cock is turned the whole distance during either its direct or retrograde movement alone; hence a smaller number of barrels can be fired by this arrangement than can by any other previously used.

In the pistol represented in the accompanying drawings, for example, there are only four barrels; but as few as three can be fired by this device with the same certainty as six can by those hitherto employed for the purpose.

What I claim as my invention, and desire to secure by Letters Patent, is—

The combination of the cocking and spring levers with the double ratchet-wheel on the revolving hammer, substantially in the manner herein set forth.

CHRISTIAN SHARPS.

Witnesses:
P. H. WATSON,
E. S. RENWICK.

C. SHARPS.
Breech-Loading Fire-Arm.

No. 5,763.

Patented Sept. 12, 1848.

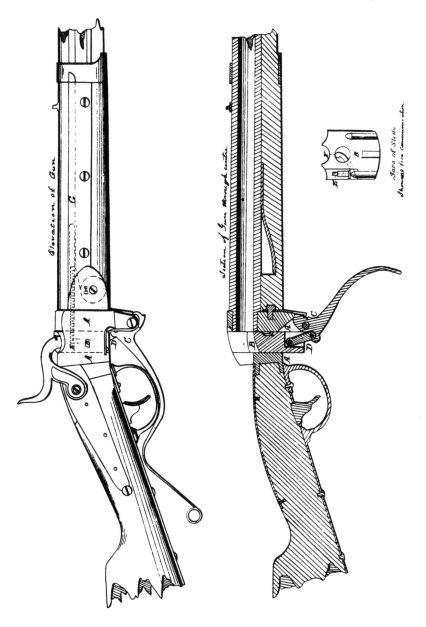

UNITED STATES PATENT OFFICE.

CHRISTIAN SHARPS, OF CINCINNATI, OHIO.

SLIDING BREECH-PIN AND SELF-CAPPING GUN.

Specification forming part of Letters Patent No. **5,763,** dated September 12, 1848.

To all whom it may concern:

Be it known that I, CHRISTIAN SHARPS, of Cincinnati, in the county of Hamilton and State of Ohio, have invented a new and Improved Breech-Loading and Self-Capping Rifle-Gun; and I do hereby declare that the following is a full and exact description thereof.

The nature of my invention consists in the following particulars, namely: its construction to admit a cartridge being inserted in the breech of the barrel on a line with the bore; the breech-slide cutting off the cartridge; its having a stationary tube with many caps, and the caps being put upon the nipple by the moving of the sliding breech.

To enable others skilled in the art to make and use my invention, I will proceed to describe its construction and operation.

I construct my gun by screwing, brazing, or welding a piece of steel or iron to the end of a rifle-barrel. It should be at least two inches square, with a projection on the under front part. This piece of steel or iron being for a supporter and receiver of the sliding breech, will be the breech-supporter A. It has a mortise through it which will admit of a slide, B, one inch and three-quarters wide and three-quarters of an inch thick, to move in a perpendicular position, and is at right angles with the bore. The slide B is connected with the lever C by a stirrup, D. The lever then being secured by a pin passing through it and the projection on the under front part of the breech-supporter A, will cause the slide to open and close the breech-bore of the barrel when the lever C is moved back and forth. The barrel is made fast to the supporter A within one-eight of an inch of its upper surface. The supporter A and connecting parts back of the slide B must have a half-round groove cut in the top of them, as shown in the section on a line with the under surface of the bore, and at the same time leaving a sufficient bearing for the slide to withstand the resistance when the gun is discharged. The slide B contains the cap-nipple E and fire-communication F, and has a shearing-edge to cut off the cartridge when the slide is moved across the bore. The bore of the barrel is counterbored to receive the length of the cartridge, leaving a small portion thereof projecting for the slide to cut off and expose the powder to the communication.

There is a tube, G, attached to the side of the barrel some eight or ten inches long, with one end passing through a portion of the supporter A and half across the mortise parallel with the barrel. This tube has a cross-hole at the end, which will admit the cap-nipple to pass up sufficiently to carry a cap above the surface of the tube G when the gun is breeched. There is a small cord attached to a follower, I, which passes through the stationary tube G, the cord winding round a cylinder, H, inclosing a watch-spring. This cylinder runs on a stud made fast to a metallic plate, which is placed under the tube G against the supporter A, and which plate is made fast to the front part of the stock. The gun-stock is made in two pieces, the one joining the front part of the supporter A, the other the back. The back part of the stock may be secured by break-off iron plates secured to the supporter A in such a manner as to come on the upper and lower surfaces of the stock and be made fast in the ordinary way, the lock being the common back-action. The lever C, that moves the slide B, will be on the guard when the gun is breeched, and has a small spring that will hold it against the guard, and also retain it in its proper position when open, operating as the spring of a pocket-knife. The remainder of the gun may be finished in the ordinary manner.

To charge the stationary tube G with caps, the follower I must be drawn to the mouth of the tube G, which is done with the rod of the gun; then insert the caps and replace the follower in the tube. This will always exert a pressure on the caps, which will cause one to occupy the cross-hole in the tube G when the nipple is withdrawn, and as the nipple is returned it takes on the cap.

To use this gun, prepare a cartridge by making a paper tube nearly the size of the counterbore of the barrel. Into one end of the tube put a ball with a patch drawn over it. The paper tube may pass over the folds of the patch and be tied with a thread. This paper tube, being then charged with powder, may be closed by tying. Now, by moving the lever forward the breech of the barrel will be opened to receive the cartridge. In the meantime a cap will be standing in the cross-hole of the tube G. The whole operation then consists in mply inserting the cartridge and returning e lever to its place, the gun being now load-d and capped.

The advantages this gun has over all breech-ading guns is that it loads at the breech and aves the whole charge in the main barrel; so, the moving part of the breech being but ttle exposed to the fire, it does not expand g; and, again, the moving part of the breech eing performed by a lever with high power, made to close the barrel perfectly tight, and o accident can occur by loading, as the cap oes not reach the hammer of the lock until e breech is perfectly secure. At the same me the gun is not liable to become choked ith dirt, in consequence of the balls being atched, which performs a wiping operation ach time the gun is discharged.

What I claim as my invention, and desire to ecure by Letters Patent, is—

1. The combination of the sliding breech with the barrel, the breech-supporter, and the stock in such a manner that when the sliding breech is forced down the breech-bore will be so exposed as to enable it to receive a cartridge on a line with the bore, and when the sliding breech is forced up it will shear off the rear end of the cartridge, so as to expose the powder to the fire-communication, and will firmly and securely close the breech-bore, substantially as herein set forth.

2. The combination of the cap-nipple with the sliding breech, substantially in the manner and for the purpose herein set forth.

CHRISTIAN SHARPS.

Witnesses:
    Z. C. ROBBINS,
    L. WILLIAMS.

C. SHARPS.

Breech-Loading Fire-Arm.

No. 22,752.

Patented Jan. 25, 1859.

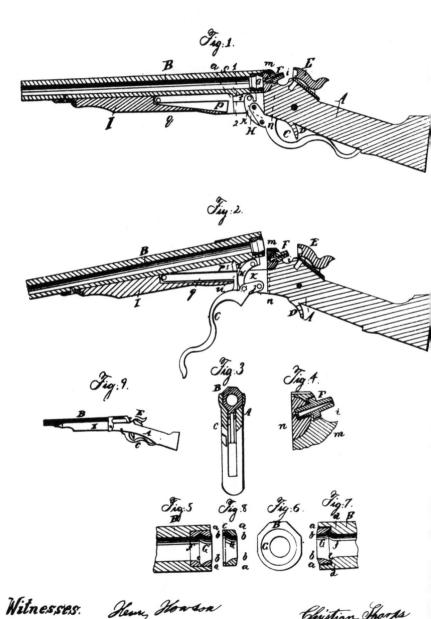

Fig: 1.

Fig: 2.

Fig: 9.

Fig: 3.

Fig: 4.

Fig: 5.

Fig: 8.

Fig: 6.

Fig: 7.

Witnesses.

Henry Howson
Henry Odione

Christian Sharps

UNITED STATES PATENT OFFICE.

CHRISTIAN SHARPS, OF PHILADELPHIA, PENNSYLVANIA.

IMPROVEMENT IN BREECH-LOADING FIRE-ARMS.

Specification forming part of Letters Patent No. 22,752, dated January 25, 1859.

o all whom it may concern:

Be it known that I, CHRISTIAN SHARPS, of city and county of Philadelphia, and State of Pennsylvania, have invented certain new and useful Improvements in Breech-Loading Fire-Arms; and I do hereby declare the following to be a full, clear, and exact description of the same, reference being had to the accompanying drawings, and to the letters of reference marked thereon.

My invention relates to that class of fire-arms in which the end of the barrel is removed from the breech for the purpose of inserting the cartridge; and my invention consists in forming on the outer end of a bush which is arranged to fit into and slide within a recess in the end of the barrel, an annular inclined projection with a sharp annular edge coinciding with the smallest portion of the bore of the bush, so that when the explosion of the cartridge takes place no obstacle may be presented to the backward movement of the bush, as fully described hereinafter. This bush has an annular termination fitting into an annular recess in the barrel, said termination being overlapped by a sharp annular projection, as fully described hereinafter, so as to prevent the penetration of any refuse matter between the end of the bush and the barrel when the discharge takes place, and so as to clear away all refuse matter which may adhere to the termination of the bush. A concave base is fitted into a concave recess in the breech in such a manner that the said base may be self-adjusting to the end of the barrel, and thereby insure an accurate fit and prevent leakage when the discharge takes place.

In order to enable others to make and use my invention, I will now proceed to describe its construction and operation.

On reference to the accompanying drawings, which form a part of this specification, Figure 1 is a longitudinal section of sufficient of a breech-loading fire-arm to illustrate my improvements; Fig. 2, a sectional view with the barrel elevated; Fig. 3, a transverse section on the line 1 2, Fig. 1; Fig. 4, an enlarged view of the self-adjusting base of the breech; Figs. 5, 6, 7, and 8, enlarged views of the inner end of the barrel with the sliding bush; Fig. 9, an exterior view of Fig. 1, drawn to a reduced scale.

Similar letters refer to similar parts throughout the several views.

A is the stock of the fire-arm; B, the barrel; C, the trigger-guard; D, the trigger; E, the hammer, and F the nipple.

As the hammer and trigger, as well as the appliances connected therewith, form no part of my present invention, a description of them will be unnecessary.

A recess is formed in the rear end of the barrel for the reception of the bush G. (See Figs. 5, 6, 7, and 8. The outer end of this bush forms an annular inclined projection, the sharp edge of which extends beyond the barrel, the inclination commencing at the outer edge, *a*, which coincides, or nearly so, with the end of the barrel, and terminates at the sharp annular cutting-edge *b*, which coincides with the smallest part of the bore of the bush. From the latter point the curved interior of the bush gradually increases in diameter, the curve meeting the straight annular projection *c*, Fig. 8, in which the bush terminates.

An annular recess, *d*, is formed in the interior of the barrel, for the reception of the annular projection *c* on the inner end of the bush. The bore of the barrel near its inner end, *f*, increases in diameter with a gentle curve and terminates at the sharp edge of the annular projection *e*, by which the recess *d* is bounded on the inside.

Instead of the recess *d* and projection *e* forming a part of the barrel, as in Fig. 7, they may be formed by a metal bush driven tight into the barrel, as seen in Fig. 5.

By the above-described arrangement the requisite enlarged chamber is formed in the end of the barrel for the reception of the cartridge, and for the expansion of the gases when the explosion takes place. The nipple F is screwed into a convex block, *n*, which fits into a recess of corresponding form in the breech *m*. Both the nipple and the block are maintained in their proper position in respect to the breech by a collar, *i*, on said nipple, the collar fitting into a recess in the breech, and the said recess being sufficiently large to allow the block *n* a slight rolling movement only in any direction within its socket. The collar *i* is concave on the inside, and fits against a convex bearing in the breech, so that the nipple may follow the movement of the block, which thus assumes the character of a self-adjusting base for the breech. The end of the trigger-guard C is hung to a pin, *j*, which passes through the stock and through a recess, *k*, formed in the stock, for the reception of the end of the trigger-guard and of the rod H, one end of which is jointed to the guard, and the opposite end to a projection, *t*, underneath and near the end of the barrel. A rod, *q*, which projects from the stock, is jointed to a projection on the under side of the barrel, which is thus allowed to vibrate to a limited extent on the end of the rod. A shoulder, *s*, on the under side of the barrel, as well as the projection *t*, fits against a shoulder on the stock and into the openings *k* when the barrel is down. When the barrel is raised to the position shown in Fig. 2, the cartridge may be readily inserted. When the trigger-guard is drawn toward the stock, and the barrel consequently brought down, the shoulder *s*, fitting against the shoulder *u*, and the annular projection *b* of the bush G bearing against the self-adjusting base *n* of the breech, the fire-arm is ready for being discharged. The instant the explosion takes place a momentary outward impulse will be imparted to the bush G, and at the same time the breech will yield to a slight extent. The bush being thus forced against the breech will form a joint, the accuracy and tightness of which is rendered certain by the sharp annular projection on the bush and by the self-adjustability of the base *n*. Should the end of the bush which bears against the breech be flat, the gases at the moment of the explosion would tend to penetrate between the flat end of the bush and the breech, and thus have an area to press against sufficient to counteract the tendency of the bush to move outward; hence the advantage of the sharp annular projection *b* coinciding with the smallest portion of the bore of the bush. This sharp projection has the further advantage of being enabled at the instant of the explosion to cut through any obstacles that may be presented on the breech. It will thus be seen that the gases cannot escape between the end of the barrel and the breech—the point which in other breech-loading fire-arms is apt

to be leaky, and consequently to detract from the explosive effect of the cartridge. Particles of dirt, too, are apt to collect in the chamber at the end of the barrel, and these would penetrate between the end of the bush and the collar of the barrel at the time of the explosion, and consequent outward movement of the bush, should the bush be made flat at the end, and these particles would of course prevent the bush from returning to its proper position after the explosion takes place, thus presenting an obstacle to the accurate fit of the barrel against the breech. The arrangement illustrated in Figs. 5, 6, 7, and 8 obviates this difficulty, for as the sharp edge of the annular lip *e* on the barrel overhangs the inside of the annular projection *c* of the bush at all times, it must prevent the particles of dirt from entering the annular recess *d* of the barrel, and whatever refuse matter may collect on the uncovered portion of the inside of the annular projection *c* of the bush at the moment of the explosion and outward movement of the bush that refuse matter will, on the restoration of the bush to its position, be scraped off by the sharp-edged annular projection *c* of the barrel.

I claim and desire to secure by Letters Patent—

1. Forming on the outer end of the sliding bush G, as the sole bearing-point against the breech, an annular inclined projection with a sharp annular edge, *b*, coinciding with the smallest portion of the bore of the said bush as and for the purpose herein set forth.

2. The annular termination *e* of the sliding bush fitting into an annular recess, *d*, formed in the barrel and overlapped by the sharp edged annular projection *e*, substantially as herein set forth, and for the purpose specified

3. The convex base *n*, as fitted into a concave socket in the breech, so as to form a self adjusting base for the end of the barrel.

In testimony whereof I have signed my name to this specification in the presence of two subscribing witnesses.

CHRISTIAN SHARPS.

Witnesses:
HENRY HOWSON,
HORACE SEE.

C. SHARPS.

Revolver.

No. 22,753.

Patented Jan. 25, 1859.

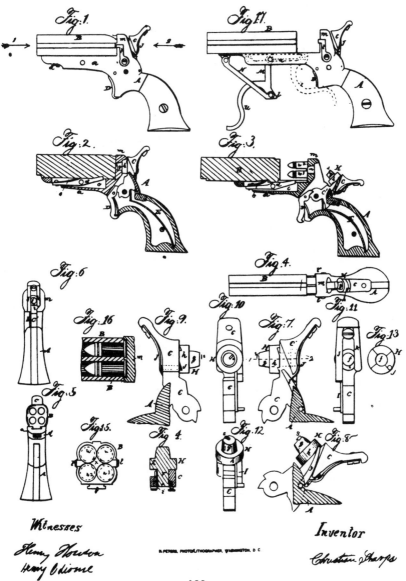

Witnesses

Henry Houston

Henry Odiorne

B. PETERS, PHOTOLITHOGRAPHER, WASHINGTON, D.C.

Inventor

Christian Sharps

133

UNITED STATES PATENT OFFICE.

CHRISTIAN SHARPS, OF PHILADELPHIA, PENNSYLVANIA.

IMPROVEMENT IN BREECH-LOADING REPEATING FIRE-ARMS.

Specification forming part of Letters Patent No. **22,753**, dated January 25, 1859.

To all whom it may concern:

Be it known that I, CHRISTIAN SHARPS, of the city and county of Philadelphia and State of Pennsylvania, have invented certain new and useful Improvements in Breech-Loading Repeating Fire-Arms; and I do hereby declare the following to be a full, clear, and exact description of the same, reference being had to the accompanying drawings, and to the letters of reference marked thereon.

My invention relates to improvements in breech-loading fire-arms in which one particular description of ammunition only is used—namely, a cartridge consisting of a case containing the powder, with a bullet attached to one end of the case and an enlargement or projection at the opposite end for containing the detonating material.

My improvements consist, first, in discharging in succession a number of the above cartridges by means of a projection caused to revolve by the movement of the hammer, the cartridges being so arranged in respect to the projection that the latter shall strike the edge of each cartridge in succession; second, in a sliding barrel-block with two or more bores, in combination with certain spring-clips attached to the stock, and so arranged in respect to the cartridges that the latter may be withdrawn simultaneously from their respective bores on moving the barrel from the breech.

In order to enable others to make and use my invention, I will now proceed to describe its construction and operation.

On reference to the accompanying drawings, which form a part of this specification, Figure 1 is an exterior side view of my improved breech-loading repeating-pistol; Fig. 2, a longitudinal section of the same with the hammer down; Fig. 3, a longitudinal section of the same with the hammer cocked and the barrel-block slid out; Fig. 4, a plan view; Fig. 5, an end view looking in the direction of the arrow 1, Fig. 1; Fig. 6, an end view looking in the direction of the arrow 2, Fig. 1; Fig. 7, a detached view (drawn to an enlarged scale) of the hammer when down; Fig. 8, the same view of the hammer when cocked; Fig. 9, a side view of the hammer the reverse of that illustrated in Fig. 7; Fig. 10, a front view of the hammer; Fig. 11, a rear view of the hammer; Fig. 12, a front view of Fig. 8; Fig. 13, a rear view of the revolving nipple, showing the notches and retaining-pin; Fig. 14, a sectional plan of the hammer with its revolving nipple on the line 1 2, Fig. 7; Fig. 15, an end view, showing the end of the barrel-block with its four cartridges, all having been discharged except one; Fig. 16, a sectional view of the barrel through two of the bores and a part of the breech; Fig. 17, an exterior view of the pistol, showing a lever arrangement for moving the barrel in and out.

Similar letters refer to similar parts throughout the several views.

A is the stock of the pistol, and B the barrel-block, which in this instance has two bores in the width of the block and two in the depth, the bores at equal distances from a point, in the center of the block, as seen in Figs. and 15.

The under side of the barrel-block is made perfectly straight and true, so as to fit accurately on the edges of the projecting portion *a* of the stock, which has grooves adapted to receive the lips of the projection *b* on the under side of the barrel-block, this projection being of such a form as to retain the block in close contact with the projection *a* of the stock and to allow the former to slide freely longitudinally on the latter, but so that the one can have no vertical or lateral motion independent of the other.

In the projecting portion *a* of the block, and between the grooves for receiving the lips of the projection *b*, a chamber or recess, *c*, is formed, and within the same is hung a catch-lever, *d*, having two arms, the end of one arm fitting into a notch on the under side of the barrel-block, where it is retained by a spring *e*, attached to the end of the opposite arm of the lever and bearing against the under side of the barrel-block.

The arm of the lever to which the spring is attached projects so far through an opening in the end of the projection *a* of the stock as to be easily elevated by applying the finger to it, thereby depressing the opposite arm and releasing the barrel-block, which can then be slid outward until its notch comes in contact with the point of the spring, as seen in Fig. 3.

C is the hammer, D the trigger, and E the mainspring, of the pistol, all being arranged within a recess formed in the stock, the two former being hung to pins passing transversely through the stock, and the spring bearing with its point in an angular recess formed in the hammer.

H is the revolving nipple, the pin *f* of which (see Fig. 14) fits snugly, but so as to turn freely, in an orifice in the hammer C, to which it is confined on one side by a collar, *h*, which forms a part of the nipple, and on the opposite side by a nut, *i*, which fits into a recess in the rear of the hammer, and which screws onto or is otherwise secured to the end of the pin *f*.

On the inside of the collar *h* of the revolving nipple, and where it bears against the hammer, are cut four radial notches, (see Fig. 13,) at equal distances apart, and inclined on one side and abrupt on the other.

A pin, *j*, Figs. 9 and 13, passes freely through an orifice in the hammer, and is caused by means of a spring, *k*, to bear with its point against the inside of the collar *h* of the revolving nipple, where it rests at the deepest point of one of the radial notches of the collar, and thus serves to retain the revolving nipple H in a given position prior to its being moved therefrom by the cocking of the hammer, as hereinafter described.

To a pin secured to the stock is hung a catch or "hand," I, the point of which is adapted to the radial notches on the collar H, in gear with one or other of which it is maintained by a spring, J, secured to the back of the hammer. This hand is so arranged in respect to the notches that it rests, when the hammer is down, on a projection on the stock, the point being then clear of the said notches. When the hammer, however, is in the act of being drawn back, the rear of the collar *h* is brought in contact with the hand, the point of the latting into one of the radial notches and turning the rotating nipple, so that when the hammer has reached the position of full-cock the nipple will have been turned one-quarter of its circumference round, and in this position it is retained by the pin *j* during the descent of the hammer, when the hand I, by the action of the spring J, recovers its former stationary position on the stock until the hammer is again cocked, when the rotating nipple will be moved another quarter of its circumference round, as before.

In the breech *m*, which projects from and forms a part of the stock, is a circular opening, *n*, for the free admission of the end *q* of the revolving nipple H when the hammer is down, the center of the opening *n* coinciding with that of the nipple, and the centers of both coinciding with the central point, *x*, Figs. 5 and 15, of the barrel-block.

On the face of the end of the rotating nipple is a projection, *s*, radiating from the center of the nipple and terminating at the edge of the face. This projection is the immediate cause of the ignition of the detonating substance contained in the enlarged end of the cartridge.

It should be understood that one particular class of cartridges only is used in connection with my improved pistol. These cartridges consist of a capsule or casing of thin metal containing powder, a portion of the bullet being inserted and secured to one end, and the opposite end being enlarged so as to form a collar or projection for preventing the cartridge from entering too far into the bore of the barrel and for containing the detonating material.

In the breech *m* four circular recesses are formed, coinciding with the four bores, and into these recesses fit the enlarged ends of the cartridges when the barrel-block is brought home to the breech. The rear of each cartridge is thus covered by the breech, excepting a small portion of the edge, which is exposed at the central opening, *n*, as best observed on reference to Fig. 15.

On each side of the stock is secured a spring-catch, *t*, the ends of the catches being bent so as to project inward in front of the breech, a slight incision on each side of the barrel-block preventing the latter, when moved toward the breech, from interfering with the points of said catches, which are so constructed and situated that when the barrel, with its cartridges, is brought up to the breech the bent end of one catch shall pass between the enlarged ends of the upper and lower cartridges and the barrel on one side and between the enlarged ends of the upper and lower cartridges and the barrel on the opposite side, as seen in Fig. 15, the points of the clips assuming this position without any other aid than the pressure of the enlarged ends of the cartridges against them when the barrel is brought home to the breech.

The barrel-block being slid forward to the position shown in Fig. 3, the hammer being cocked, and the cartridges being inserted into their respective bores, the block is pushed up to the breech, the clips *t t* catch under the enlarged ends of the cartridges, the catch-lever *d* assumes its position in the notch on the under side of the barrel-block, when the pistol is ready for firing.

When the trigger is drawn the projection *s* on the face of the hammer will strike on the edge of the enlarged portion of one cartridge only and cause the same to be discharged. When the hammer is again cocked, prior to a second discharge, the nipple must have turned, as hereinbefore described, one quarter round, and the projection *s*, on account of its eccentricity with the center of rotation of the nipple, must consequently have been turned away from the cartridge upon which it acted last, and have assumed a position ready to act upon a second cartridge, and this position of the projection *s* changes every time the hammer is thrown back, each cartridge being acted upon in succession until the whole are discharged. The end of the catch-lever *d* which projects through the end of the stock is then elevated and the barrel released and pushed forward. In doing this the catches *t t* maintain their hold on the enlarged ends of the spent cartridges, the latter being withdrawn from their respective bores and dropping to the ground. The pistol is now in a condition to receive a second supply of cartridges.

In adapting my improvements to the larger class of pistols it will facilitate the operation of loading to apply an extra power in sliding the barrel-block in and out. This is effected by the arrangement illustrated in Fig. 17. A lever, M, of which the trigger-guard *n* forms a part, is hung to a pin in the projecting portion *a* of the stock, and to this lever is hinged one end of the rod N, the opposite end of which is hinged to a projection on the under side of the barrel-block B. An angular projection is formed on the lever M, and this projection is adapted to a notch in the under side of the barrel-block and near the rear of the same. When the latter is slid out from the breach the above-named parts will assume the position illustrated in the figure. When the barrel has to be brought up to the breech the operator draws the lever M to the position shown in dotted lines, when the projection V is fitted into the notch of the barrel and the bent portion of the lever assumes the character and duty of an ordinary trigger-guard.

It will thus be seen that by the above-described arrangement two duties are performed—the sliding in and out of the barrel-block and the retention and release of the same.

Having now described the nature of my invention and the manner in which the same is carried into effect, I wish it to be understood that I do not desire to confine myself to the use of a barrel-block with four bores or to the precise devices herein described for altering the position of the projection *s*, inasmuch as a barrel-block with more or less than four bores may be used in connection with my improvement, and as different devices may be used for changing the position of the said projection; but

I claim and desire to secure by Letters Patent—

1. Exploding in succession a number of cartridges of the class herein described by means of a projection caused to revolve by the movement of the hammer when the said cartridges are so arranged in respect to the said projection that the latter shall strike the edge only of each cartridge in succession, as herein set forth.

2. The catches *t t*, so arranged on the stock in respect to the bores of the barrel-block that on moving the latter from the breech they may be the means of withdrawing the whole of the cartridges simultaneously from their respective bores, as herein set forth.

In testimony whereof I have signed my name to this specification in the presence of two subscribing witnesses.

CHRISTIAN SHARPS.

Witnesses:
HENRY HOWSON,
HORACE SEE.

C. SHARPS.

Revolver.

No. 30,765. **Patented Nov. 27, 1860.**

Fig: 1.

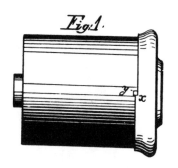

Fig. 2

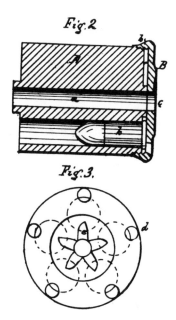

Fig. 3.

Witnesses

Chas Howson

Charles E Foster

Henry Howson

Atty for C. Sharps

N. PETERS, PHOTO-LITHOGRAPHER, WASHINGTON, D. C.

UNITED STATES PATENT OFFICE.

CHRISTIAN SHARPS, OF PHILADELPHIA, PENNSYLVANIA.

IMPROVEMENT IN THE REVOLVING BLOCKS OF REVOLVING FIRE-ARMS.

Specification forming part of Letters Patent No. **30,765**, dated November 27, 1860.

To all whom it may concern:

Be it known that I, CHRISTIAN SHARPS, of the city of Philadelphia and State of Pennsylvania, have invented a new and useful Improvement in Revolving Fire-Arms; and I do hereby declare the following to be a full, clear, and exact description of the same, reference being had to the accompanying drawings, and to the letters of reference marked thereon.

My invention relates to an improvement in that class of revolving breech-blocks which are made in detachable pieces for the purpose of inclosing the enlarged ends of metallic cartridges and allowing the spent cartridges to be readily withdrawn; and my improvement consists of a breech-block and a detachable cap for the same, the latter being so adapted to the former that when the two are fitted together they shall become temporarily a permanent portion of each other, the cap being incapable of yielding to the reaction caused by the explosion of the cartridge, as in other breech-blocks made of detachable pieces, which separate when the discharge takes place, and thereby interfere with the ready revolving of the block.

In order to enable others skilled in the art to make and use my invention, I will now proceed to describe its construction and operation.

On reference to the accompanying drawings, which form a part of this specification, Figure 1 is an exterior view of the breech-block of a revolver with my improvement; Fig. 2, a longitudinal section of Fig 1, and Fig. 3 a rear end view of the revolving breech.

Similar letters refer to similar parts throughout the several views.

A represents the breech-block of a revolving fire-arm, the said block having the usual orifice, *a*, for the reception of the breech-pin, and having in the present instance five bores, which are adapted to receive the ordinary metallic cartridges, *b*, circular recesses being cut in the end of the block for the reception of the flanges or enlargements formed at the rear ends of cartridges of this class. On the edge of the block, at the rear end of the same, is cut a screw-thread, adapted to a similar thread cut on the inside of the flange *b* of the cap B, which has a central opening, *c*, forming a continuation of the opening *a* in the block for the reception of the breech-pin. The cap has also a series of openings, *d d*, corresponding in number to that of the bores in the block. When the cap is screwed to its proper place on the end of the block the enlarged ends of the cartridges are entirely inclosed, with the exception of such portion of each cartridge as is of necessity exposed at each opening *d*, through which the end of the hammer must pass for the purpose of striking the end of the cartridge and exploding the detonating material contained within the same.

In order that the cap, on being replaced after withdrawal, may always assume its proper position on the block, a collar or catch, *x*, Fig. 4 is formed on the flange *b* of the cap, and this catch bears against a stop, *y*, attached to or otherwise formed on the block, when the cap has been turned to its proper position, so that each hole *d* may expose a suitable portion of the surface of the enlarged end of one of the cartridges. The back of the cap is furnished with proper notches, *e*, for receiving the end of the dog by which the block is revolved during the cocking of the hammer.

I am aware that the breech-block of a revolver has been heretofore made in detachable pieces, so as to inclose the enlarged ends of metallic cartridges and at the same time to allow for their withdrawal. The pieces composing the block, however, have been hitherto held together by the frame of the fire-arm only, so that the explosion of the cartridge causes that separation of the pieces. This I have been desirous of avoiding, inasmuch as one portion of the block on the discharge of the cartridge is driven hard against one side and the other hard against the opposite side of the frame within which the block has to revolve. At the same time the expansion of the metal case of the discharged cartridge prevents the pieces composing the block from recovering their proper relative position. In other words, the block becomes so jammed as to render it a matter of great difficulty to turn it by the cocking of the hammer.

In my improvement the cap, when adjusted to its place, becomes a permanent part of the block and effectually resists the reaction caused by the explosion of the cartridges. At the same me it affords every facility for the withdrawal of the spent cartridges.

It will be evident that in place of the screw-thread other well-known mechanical appliances may be used for attaching the cap to the block for the purpose of arriving at the result desired.

Without claiming broadly a revolving breech-block furnished with a detachable cap, I claim as my invention and desire to secure by Letters Patent—

The breech-block A and detachable cap B, when the latter is so adapted to the former that when the two are fitted together they shall become temporarily a permanent portion of each other, as and for the purpose herein set forth.

In testimony whereof I have signed my name to this specification in the presence of two subscribing witnesses.

CHRISTIAN SHARPS.

Witnesses:
HENRY HOWSON,
JOHN WHITE.

C. SHARPS.

Sight for Fire-Arms.

No. ⎰ 1,895. ⎱
   ⎱ 32,899. ⎰

Patented July 23, 1861.

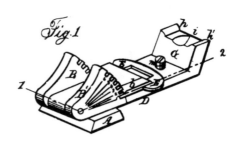

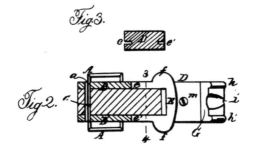

UNITED STATES PATENT OFFICE.

CHRISTIAN SHARPS, OF PHILADELPHIA, PENNSYLVANIA.

IMPROVEMENT IN ADJUSTABLE BACK SIGHTS FOR FIRE-ARMS.

Specification forming part of Letters Patent No. **32,899,** dated July 23, 1861.

To all whom it may concern:

Be it known that I, CHRISTIAN SHARPS, of Philadelphia, Pennsylvania, have invented an Adjustable Sight for Fire-Arms; and I do hereby declare the following to be a full, clear, and exact description of the same, reference being had to the accompanying drawings, and to the letters of reference marked thereon.

My invention consists of a movable arm having a notched projection and a sliding plate, in combination with certain notched flanges, the whole being constructed and operating, substantially as described hereinafter, so as to form a sight which can be readily and accurately adjusted to suit any desired range.

In order to enable others skilled in the art to make and use my invention, I will now proceed to describe its construction and operation.

On reference to the accompanying drawings, which form a part of this specification, Figure 1 is a perspective view of my improved adjustable sight for fire-arms; Fig. 2, a sectional plan on the line 1 2, Fig. 1; and Fig. 3, a transverse section on the line 3 4, Fig. 2.

Similar letters refer to similar parts throughout the several views.

A is a dovetailed plate adapted to a dovetailed recess cut across the top of the barrel of the fire-arm to which my improved sight is to be secured. Two flanges or ribs, B and B', are attached to or form a part of this plate A, and between these flanges an arm, D, fits snugly, but so as to vibrate freely on a pin, a, which passes through both flanges and arm. The rear edge of each flange is convex, as shown in Fig. 1, and forms part of a circle f which the center of the pin a is the center. The arm D is increased in thickness at b, at which point the arm is wider than at that portion which fits between the flanges B and B', so that a shoulder is formed on each side of the arm, one shoulder being nearly in contact with and adapted to the convex edge of the flange B, and the other shoulder to the convex edge of the flange B'. On each side of the thicker portion of the arm D is cut a recess, (best observed on reference to Fig. 3,) and in one recess fits the projection c, and in the other recess the projection c', of the sliding plate E,

the ends of these projections being adapted to fit into notches cut in the convex edges of the flanges B and B'.

The plate A is secured to the barrel of the fire-arm at a suitable distance from the breech toward which the arm D projects, the lateral position of the sight on the barrel being such that the notch i on the top of the projection G of the arm D shall be central with the bore of the barrel, so that a correct aim can be taken if the altitude of this notch be properly regulated to suit the distance at which the load has to take effect. It will be observed that in this instance each of the flanges B and B' has six notches, each notch being numbered, and each number indicating the position to which the sight must be adjusted in order that the load may take effect at a given range.

In adjusting the sight the operator grasps the sliding plate E between his finger and thumb at the projections f f and draws the plate back until it comes in contact with a stud, m, on the arm D, when the ends of the projections c and c' of the plate will be withdrawn from the notches in the flanges B and B', and the arm D will be at liberty to be raised and lowered at pleasure. After examining the figures opposite the notches and selecting that notch to which he desires to adjust the arm, the operator moves the latter until the ends of the projections c and c' coincide with the desired notches, when he moves the sliding plate E until the projections penetrate these notches. After this the plate D is locked and the required adjustment accomplished.

I claim as my invention and desire to secure by Letters Patent—

The movable arm D, with its notched projection G and sliding plate E, in combination with the notched flanges B and B', the whole being constructed and operating substantially as and for the purpose herein set forth.

In testimony whereof I have signed my name to this specification in the presence of two subscribing witnesses.

CHRISTIAN SHARPS.

Witnesses:
 HENRY HOWSON,
 CHARLES E. FOSTER.

C. SHARPS.

Gun-Lock.

No. { 2,542. / 33.546. }

Patented Oct. 22, 1861.

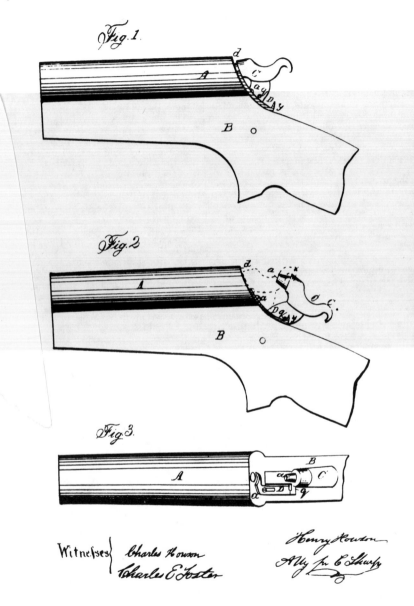

Fig. 1.

Fig. 2.

Fig. 3.

Witnesses{ Charles Howson
Charles E. Foster

Henry Howson
Atty. for C. Sharps

UNITED STATES PATENT OFFICE.

CHRISTIAN SHARPS, OF PHILADELPHIA, PENNSYLVANIA.

IMPROVEMENT IN HAMMER-GUARDS TO FIRE-ARMS.

Specification forming part of Letters Patent No. **23,516**, dated October 22, 1861.

To all whom it may concern:

Be it known that I, CHRISTIAN SHARPS, of Philadelphia, Pennsylvania, have invented a Hammer-Guard for Fire-Arms; and I do hereby declare the following to be a full, clear, and exact description of the same, reference being had to the accompanying drawings, and to the letters of reference marked thereon.

My invention consists of a device, described hereinafter, for preventing the unintentional discharge of fire-arms used for the discharge of metallic cartridges.

In order to enable others skilled in the art to make and use my invention, I will now proceed to describe its construction and operation.

On reference to the accompanying drawings, which form a part of this specification, Figures 1 and 2 are side views of sufficient of a fire-arm to illustrate my improved hammer-guard, and Fig. 2 a ground plan.

A represents a portion of the barrel, and B a portion of the stock, of a fire-arm, C being the hammer, which is connected with a lock and trigger arranged in the usual manner, the hammer being provided with a nipple, *a*, of a proper form for striking against and exploding that class of cartridges which consist of a metal casing having a bullet at one end and a collar or enlargement at the opposite end, containing the detonating material, between which and the bullet intervenes the charge of powder.

Accidents frequently take place in using fire-arms in which cartridges of this class are employed, especially when the hammer is down and its nipple in contact or nearly in contact with the collar of the cartridge containing the detonating material, for on any sudden jar being imparted to the fire-arm the nipple of the hammer is apt to penetrate the collar of the cartridge or to be brought into such forcible contact therewith as to cause an unintentional explosion. The same remarks will apply to fire-arms in which ordinary caps are employed.

It will be observed that the rear, *d*, of the breech and part of the stock are curved, the curve of one meeting that of the other, so as to form a continuous concavity. On this concavity I fit a curved strip, D, of metal, having an oblong slot, through which passes a set-screw, *a*, into the breech, so that the strip can have a limited reciprocating movement in one direction, only—namely, that of the curve against which it bears. This strip, which I have termed a "hammer-guard," is bent at one end to the form represented in the plan view Fig. 3, so that when the guard is moved upward it will intervene between the rear of the breech and a collar, *x*, on the hammer, when the latter is down, thus preventing the nipple from being brought into contact with the collar of the cartridge. The side of the hammer is furnished with a pin, *q*, and the lower end of the guard D with a projection, *y*, the pin and projection being so situated in respect to each other that on drawing back the hammer to the position of full-cock the pin *q* will strike against the projection *y* and move the guard D downward, so that its upper end will be clear of the collar *x* of the hammer when the latter descends.

As long as the fire-arm is not required for use, care is taken to move the guard to the position shown in Fig. 1, its upper end, as before remarked, intervening between the rear of the breech and the collar *x* of the hammer, thus preventing an unintentional discharge of the load; but when the fire-arm is required for use the guard is moved downward by the movement of the hammer itself, so that the nipple can take the desired effect on the cartridge.

I do not desire to claim, broadly, an adjustable obstruction for preventing the hammer of a fire-arm from discharging the load; but

I claim as my invention and desire to secure by Letters Patent

The curved guard D, with its projection *y*, in combination with the hammer C, its collar *x*, and pin *q*, the whole being arranged on a fire-arm for discharging metallic cartridges, as and for the purposes herein set forth.

In testimony whereof I have signed my name to this specification in the presence of two subscribing witnesses.

CHRISTIAN SHARPS.

Witnesses:
HENRY HOWSON,
JOHN WHITE.

C. SHARPS.
Breech-Loading Fire-Arm.

No. { 2,603,
33,607. }

Patented Oct. 29, 1861.

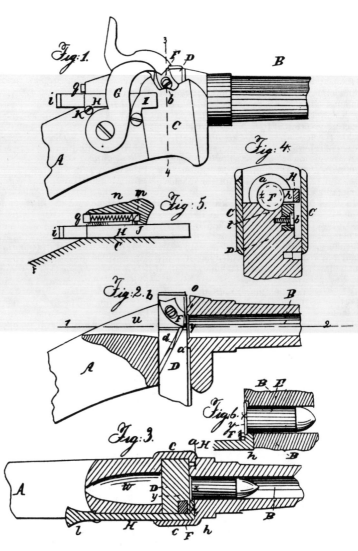

Witnesses Charles E. Foster
Chas Howson

Henry Howson
Atty for C. Sharps

N. PETERS, PHOTO-LITHOGRAPHER, WASHINGTON, D.C.

United States Patent Office

CHRISTIAN SHARPS, OF PHILADELPHIA, PENNSYLVANIA.

IMPROVEMENT IN BREECH-LOADING FIRE-ARMS.

Specification forming part of Letters Patent No. **33,607**, dated October 29, 1861.

To all whom it may concern:

Be it known that I, CHRISTIAN SHARPS, of Philadelphia, Pennsylvania, have invented certain new and useful Improvements in Breech-Loading Fire-Arms; and I do hereby declare the following to be a full, clear, and exact description of the same, reference being had to the accompanying drawings, and to the letters of reference marked thereon.

My invention relates to improvements in breech-loading fire-arms especially arranged for discharging what are generally known as metallic cartridges; and my improvements consist, first, in a vertical sliding breech, in combination with the rear of the barrel, the latter being so recessed as to receive the head of the metallic cartridge; secondly, in a movable block arranged on the sliding breech, substantially as described hereinafter, and forming a medium of communication between the hammer and the metallic cartridge for the purpose of discharging the latter; thirdly, in furnishing the bar by means of which the spent cartridge is extracted with an inclined notch so arranged in respect to the head of the metallic cartridge that when the latter is discharged a portion of the head will penetrate the notch, and thereby become so connected with the end of the bar that the extraction of the cartridge may be effected with certainty.

In order to enable others skilled in the art to make and use my invention, I will now proceed to describe its construction and operation.

On reference to the accompanying drawings, which form a part of this specification, Figure 1 is a side view of a sufficient portion of a breech-loading fire-arm to illustrate my improvements; Fig. 2, a sectional view; Fig. 3, a sectional plan on the line 1 2, Fig. 2; Fig. 4, a transverse vertical section on the line 3 4, Fig. 1; Fig. 5, a sectional view of a portion of my improvements, and Fig. 6 an enlarged sectional view of a portion of the rear end of the barrel with the metallic cartridge.

Similar letters refer to similar parts throughout the several views.

A represents part of the barrel, and B part of the stock, of the fire-arm. C being the frame which forms the junction of the stock with the barrel. In this frame is formed an opening for receiving the vertical sliding breech D, which is situated at right angles to the bore of the barrel, and which may be operated by a lever bent so as to form the trigger-guard, or by an independent lever, as seen in my patent of September 12, 1848, the front face of the sliding breech fitting snugly against the projection *a* at the rear of the barrel, as seen in Fig. 2, and this projection being recessed for the reception of the head or enlargement *x* of the metallic cartridge E. On one side of the sliding breech is a curved recess for receiving a curved block, F, which is confined to the breech by a set-screw, *b*, passing through an oblong slot in the block, so that the latter can have a limited movement in its curved recess. The lower end of the block is provided with a small projection, *y*, so situated as to coincide with a point in the rear and near one edge of the head *x* of the metallic cartridge, as seen in Fig. 3 and in the enlarged view Fig. 6, the upper end of the block being suitably formed for receiving the outer end of the hammer G. (See Fig. 1.) A spring, *d*, fastened into an inclined recess in one side of the sliding breech, serves to maintain the block F in an elevated position and its projection *y* free from contact with the metallic cartridge when the hammer is raised.

In one side of the frame C, which connects the barrel with the stock, is a recess for receiving the sliding bar H, which has at one end a head, *i*, of a proper form for being handled by the finger and thumb, and at the opposite end a projection, *h*, fitting into a recess at the rear of the barrel, the end of this projection being arranged to catch against the inside of the head *x* of the metallic cartridge, and having an inclined notch. (Best observed on reference to the enlarged view Fig. 6.)

On the upper edge of the sliding bar H is a pin, *j*, the end of which catches into a notch in a small block, *m*, the latter being arranged to slide in a chamber formed in the frame C, and containing a spiral spring, *n*, which is confined to the chamber by a set-screw or plug, *q*. The sliding bar H is maintained in its place by the plate I and set-screw K, after the removal of which and after the detachment of the hammer the bar may be withdrawn from its place.

It will be observed on reference to Fig. 4 that there is a concave depression, *t*, on the upper edges of the sliding breech, this concavity coinciding or nearly coinciding with the lower edge of the head *x* of the metallic cartridge when the breech has been depressed to its lowest point. The object of this arrangement will be rendered apparent hereinafter. It will also be seen on reference to Figs. 2 and 3, that the upper edge of the frame C, which connects the barrel with the breech, is hollowed out or cut away at w, so as to admit of the ready admission of the cartridge to its place in the rear of the barrel when the sliding breech is depressed.

Operation: After lowering the breech to the position shown in Fig. 4, the cartridge is inserted into the barrel, its head x fitting snugly into the recess of the projection a. After this the breech is raised, the hammer cocked, and the fire-arm is ready to be discharged. On releasing the hammer it will strike the curved block F, suddenly depress the same so that its projection y will pierce the edge of the head x of the metallic cartridge and explode the detonating material with which the head is filled, thereby discharging the load. It will be observed on reference to Fig. 6 that when the projection y of the block F strikes the edge of the enlargement x of the metallic cartridge E, that portion of the enlargement struck by the said projection will be driven into the inclined notch of the projection h of the sliding bar H. After discharging the load, the hammer is elevated and the sliding breech depressed to the position shown in Fig. 4, in order that the spent cartridge may be withdrawn. This is done by means of the sliding bar H, the head i of which is seized between the finger and thumb of the operator, who pulls the bar in the direction of the stock, and thereby withdraws the spent cartridge, the flange of which has by the action of the hammer become connected with the projection h of the bar H. During the extraction of the cartridge the head is guided by the concavity or depression on the upper edge of the sliding breech. After thus withdrawing the cartridge, the bar H is allowed to be moved back to its former position by the action of the spiral spring n, another cartridge is then inserted into the bore of the barrel, and the above-described movements are repeated.

I do not desire to claim, broadly, the use of a vertical sliding breech in connection with breech-loading fire-arms; but

I claim as my invention and desire to secure by Letters Patent—

1. The vertical sliding breech D, in combination with the rear of the barrel when the latter is recessed for the reception of the head x of a metallic cartridge, substantially as set forth.

2. The block F, arranged on the sliding breech substantially as set forth, and forming a medium of communication between the hammer and the metallic cartridge, for the purpose of discharging the latter, as described.

3. The inclined notch on the end of the projection h of the sliding bar H, the said notch being so arranged in respect to the head x of the metallic cartridge that when the latter is discharged a portion of the head will penetrate the notch, as set forth, for the purpose specified.

In testimony whereof I have signed my name to this specification in the presence of two subscribing witnesses.

CHRISTIAN SHARPS.

Witnesses:
JOHN WHITE,
CHARLES E. FOSTER.

C. SHARPS.
Rifling Machine.

No. 37,057.   Patented Dec. 2, 1862.

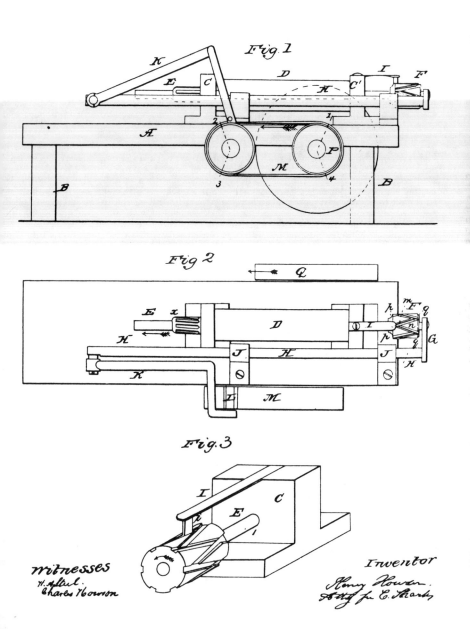

Fig. 1

Fig 2

Fig. 3

witnesses
H. Aflul.
Charles Howson

Inventor
Henry Howson.
Atty for C. Sharps

UNITED STATES PATENT OFFICE.

CHRISTIAN SHARPS, OF PHILADELPHIA, PENNSYLVANIA.

IMPROVEMENT IN RIFLING-MACHINES.

Specification forming part of Letters Patent No. **37,057**, dated December 2, 1862.

To all whom it may concern:

Be it known that I, CHRISTIAN SHARPS, of Philadelphia, Pennsylvania, have invented an Improved Rifling-Machine; and I do hereby declare the following to be a full, clear, and exact description of the same, reference being had to the accompanying drawings, and to the letters of reference marked thereon.

My invention consists of mechanism, fully described hereinafter, for imparting the desired reciprocating motion, the intermittent rotating motion, as well as the necessary spiral motion to the rod and cutter of a rifling-machine.

In order to enable others to make and use my invention, I will now proceed to describe its construction and operation.

On reference to the accompanying drawings, which form a part of this specification, Figure 1 is a side view of my improved rifling-machine; Fig. 2 a plan view, and Fig. 3 a perspective view, of part of the machine.

Similar letters refer to similar parts throughout the several views.

A is the table or platform of the machine, and is supported by suitable legs or frames, B B. To this table are secured the two standards C and C', to the former of which is attached the front end of the hollow cylinder D, the rear end of the latter being secured to the frame C'. In the interior of the cylinder are cut (in the present instance) six spiral grooves to correspond with the six grooves to be cut in the barrel of the fire-arm. A rod, E, passes through the hollow cylinder D, and this rod is enlarged near the front end, the enlarged portion fitting snugly to the bore of the cylinder, and being furnished with six inclined projections, x x, which engage into the spiral grooves cut in the said cylinder. The rod E is furnished near its rear end with a hub, F, on which are cut a number of inclined grooves, a projection, i, on the end of a spring, I, which is secured to the standard C', being arranged to engage in one or other of these grooves.

The operation and purport of the grooved hub F and spring I, with its projection i, will be fully explained hereinafter. The extreme rear of the rod E is secured by a connecting-bar, G, to the rod H, which is arranged to slide in guides J and J', secured to the table A. To a pin projecting from the rod H, at the front end of the same, is joined one end of the bent connecting rod K, the rear end of which has a pin fitting snugly, but so as to turn freely, in a box, L, secured to the endless belt M, which passes round the two pulleys N and P, the former being hung loosely to a pin secured to the under side of the table A, and the pulley P being secured to a shaft, which is arranged to turn in suitable bearings secured to the table, the outer end of this shaft being furnished with a suitable driving-pulley, Q. The barrel to be grooved is secured to the table A, and the rifling-rod to the end of the rod E. As the rifling-rod, its cutter, and other appliances connected therewith are the same as those used in other rifling-machines, it has not been deemed necessary to illustrate or describe them here. On imparting a rotary motion to the driving pulley Q in the direction of the arrow a continuous traversing motion must be communicated to the endless belt M and the box L, and consequently a reciprocating motion must be imparted from this box L, through the connecting rod K, to the rods H and E.

In ordinary rifling-machines it is usual to impart a reciprocating motion to the rifling-rod and its cutter by means of a crank motion, which causes the cutter to move at varying speeds as it traverses and acts upon the inside of the barrel—an evil avoided by my improved mode of operating the rifling rod. As the box L traverses from the point 1 to the point 2, Fig. 1, it will impart a forward movement at a uniform speed to the rifling-rod. In a like manner as the box traverses from the point 3 to the point 4 the backward movement of the rifling-rod, during which the cutter takes effect on the barrel, will be at a uniform speed. As the box traverses from the point 2 to the point 3, the forward movement of the rifling-rod is converted to a backward movement, and as the box traverses from the point 4 to the point 1 the backward movement of the rod is converted to a forward movement. It will be observed that the rod K is so bent that during its movements it will escape contact with the pulleys N and P, as well as with the endless belt. The pulley N may be rendered adjustable on the table A, so as to be removed farther from or nearer to the pulley P when a change in the length of movement of the rifling-rod is required, the length of the belt being of

148

course altered to suit the change of distance between the pulleys.

Instead of an ordinary leather belt, M, a chain with a box, L, secured to the same may be used, the pulleys being made to suit the form of the chain.

The operation of the grooved hub F and spring I with its projection i may be described as follows: Supposing this hub and spring to be absent, it will be evident that as the rod E reciprocates the inclined ribs x would invariably traverse the same grooves in the cylinder D, and consequently the cutter at the end of the rifling-rod would cut but one groove in the barrel, whereas it is necessary that the cutter should make six grooves in the barrel, and should move from one groove to the other as the rifling-rod reciprocates. In order to accomplish this it is necessary that one inclined projection, having traversed one groove in the cylinder D during one backward movement of the rod, should during the next backward movement traverse the groove nearest to that which it had previously traversed. Now, supposing the moving parts of the machine to be in the position illustrated in Figs. 1, 2, the rod E being in the act of completing its forward movement, the inclined projections x having passed from the cylinder D and being consequently free from the control of the grooves in the same, and the projection i of the spring I being situated at the junction of the two inclined grooves m and n of the hub F, now the tendency of the spring I is to cause its projection i to bear hard on the hub F, and the series of inclined grooves m are deeper at the front edge, p, of the hub than they are at the rear edge, q, whereas the grooves n are deeper at the rear edge, q, of the hub than the grooves m. When the rod E is about completing its forward movement, the projection i, seeking the deepest point, must remain in the groove m as the hub F moves forward, so that by the time the hub has passed the projection i the rod F must have turned to the extent of one-twelfth of a revolution. there being six grooves. m, and six grooves, n, in the hub. The hub F having now arrived at a point where there is a junction between a groove m and a groove n at the rear of the hub, the projection i will seek the deepest groove, which at this point is the groove n, the latter being inclined in a di

rection contrary to that of the groove m. The rod E now commences its backward movement, during which the projection i remains in the groove n, which it had previously entered, until the hub escapes from the said projection, by which time the rod E will have turned to the extent of one-twelfth of a revolution, making with the former turning through the action of the groove n one-sixth of a revolution. By the time the hub F has passed the projection i during the backward movement of the rifling-rod the projections x have entered the grooves of the cylinder D, and the rod E remains under the control of the grooves during the remainder of its backward movement and until the moving parts again arrive at the position shown in Figs. 1 and 2. It will now be seen that as the rifling-rod completes its forward and commences its backward movement it is turned to the extent of one-sixth of a revolution, and consequently that the cutter of the rifling rod must cut first one groove and then the other until the six grooves are completed in the barrel.

I claim as my invention and desire to secure by Letters Patent—

1. Imparting to the cutting-rod of a rifling-machine a reciprocating motion through the medium of an endless belt or chain, or their equivalents, and a rod connected thereto, substantially as and for the purpose herein set forth.

2. Any convenient number of projections x on the rod E, in combination with the grooved cylinder D, when each projection is caused to pass from one groove of the cylinder to the adjacent groove by the automatic devices herein described.

3. In combination with the rod E of a rifling-machine, the hub F, with its reversed inclined planes m and n, the spring I, and its projection i, the whole being arranged and operating substantially as and for the purpose herein set forth.

In testimony whereof I have signed my name to this specification in the presence of two subscribing witnesses.

CHRISTIAN SHARPS.

Witnesses:
 CHARLES E. FOSTER,
 JOHN WHITE

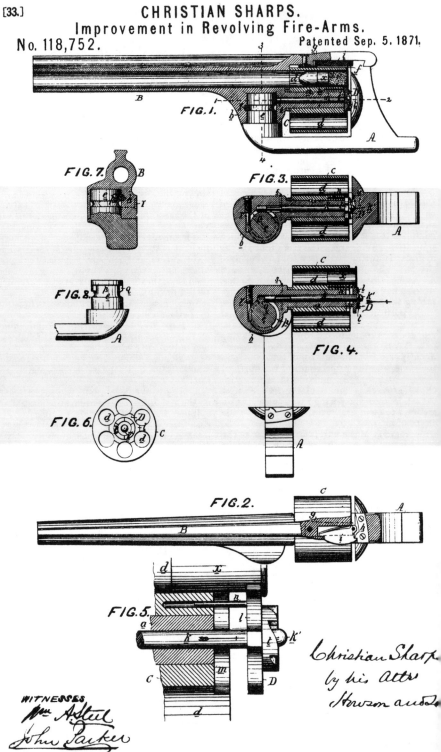

[33.]

CHRISTIAN SHARPS.
Improvement in Revolving Fire-Arms.

No. 118,752.

Patented Sep. 5. 1871.

FIG.1.

FIG.7.

FIG.3.

FIG.8.

FIG.4.

FIG.6.

FIG.2.

FIG.5.

Christian Sharps
by his Att's
Howson and

WITNESSES

Wm A. Steel
John Parker

AM. PHOTO-LITHOGRAPHIC CO N.Y. / OSBORNES PROCESS /

UNITED STATES PATENT OFFICE.

CHRISTIAN SHARPS, OF PHILADELPHIA, PENNSYLVANIA.

IMPROVEMENT IN REVOLVING FIRE-ARMS.

Specification forming part of Letters Patent No. 118,752, dated September 5, 1871.

[To a]ll whom it may concern:

[B]e it known that I, CHRISTIAN SHARPS, *of Phil[ade]lphia, county of Philadelphia, State of Penn[sylv]ania, have invented Improvements in Revolv[ing] Fire-Arms, of which the following is a speci[fica]tion:*

[M]y invention consists of certain improvements [in] revolving fire-arms, too fully explained here[afte]r to need preliminary explanation, the main [feat]ure of the said improvements being the ec[cen]tric pivoting of the barrel to the frame for [a] twofold purpose of enabling the rear end of [the] cylinder to be brought close up to and turned [out]ward from the frame without involving the [usu]al necessity of rounding off its corners, and [also] for the purpose of enabling the cartridge-[extr]actor to be readily and effectually operated.

[F]igure 1 is a longitudinal section of my im-[prov]ed revolving fire-arm; Fig. 2, a plan view [of t]he same, partly in section; Fig. 3, a sectional [plan] on the line 1 2, Fig. 1; Fig. 4, the same as [Fig.] 3, with the parts in a different position; Fig. [5, a]n enlarged view of part of Fig. 4; Fig. 6, a [plan] view of the cylinder and cartridge-extractor; [Fig.] 7, a transverse section on the line 3 4, Fig. [1; a]nd Fig. 8, a detached view of part of the fire-[arm.]

[A] represents the frame of the fire-arm, secured [to o]r forming a part of the stock; B, the barrel; C, the revolving cylinder. The latter is hung [an]d can turn freely upon a hollow stem, a, ex-[tend]ing rearward from a projection, b, beneath [the] barrel; and the said cylinder has the usual [cha]mbers d adapted for the reception of metallic [cart]ridges x, and arranged to be brought succes-[sive]ly opposite the barrel on the revolution of the [cyli]nder. The projection b, above referred to, in-[stea]d of being formed directly beneath the center [of t]he barrel, projects outward from one side of [the] same, as plainly shown in Figs. 3, 4, and 7, [and] has formed in it a cylindrical recess of en-[larg]ed diameter adapted for the reception of a [ste]m, e, of corresponding shape, secured to or [form]ing part of the frame A, and serving as a [pivo]t upon which the barrel can be turned out-[war]d from the frame, as shown in Fig. 4, when it [is de]sired to expose the rear end of the cylinder. [The] latter is retained upon the hollow stem a, but [in su]ch a manner as not to interfere with its free [mot]ion, by a light spring or catch, f, Fig. 1, se-[cure]d to the under side of the portion g of the

barrel, and bent at its outer end so as to lap over the rear edge of the cylinder. The barrel, when closed upon the frame, as shown in Figs. 1, 2, and 3, is locked to the same and prevented from accidentally turning upon the pivot e by means of a curved projection, h, of the frame, which limits the movement of the barrel in one direction, and a spring-catch, i, Fig. 2, of the barrel, adapted to a hook on the curved projection h, and which prevents any movement of the barrel in the opposite direction. The projection b is extended outward to one side of the barrel in order that the stem or pivot e may be placed eccentrically in respect to the centers of the barrel and cylinder, and the pivot is thus placed for two reasons: first, to enable the rear open end of the cylinder to be brought close up to and turned outward from the frame without risk of striking against the latter, and without involving the usual necessity of rounding off its corners; and second, to enable the said pivot to be employed as a means of operating the cartridge-extractor D. The cartridge-extractor consists of a cylindrical rod, k, adapted to an opening in the hollow stem a, and having secured to its rear end a plate, l, which forms the extractor proper, and which is fitted to a recess, m, in the rear end of the cylinder, so that when drawn in it may be flush with the exterior of the latter and extend partly into each of the chambers of the same, the edges of the said plate being curved, so that it may fit part way round each cartridge without interfering with its free introduction into the cylinder, and so that the flange of the cartridge may also overlap the rear edge of the said plate. (See Figs. 5 and 6.) As it is essential that the curved edges of the extractor-plate l should be retained in one given position opposite the chambers of the cylinder, the whole extractor is caused to revolve with, but is prevented from turning independently of, the latter by means of a rod, n, secured to the plate l and adapted to a recess in the cylinder. (See Fig. 5.) The rod k of the extractor runs forward to a point opposite the eccentric pivot e, and a portion of one side of the latter is cut away, as shown in Figs. 3, 4, 7, and 8, so as to form a groove, p, for the reception of the rod k, and an abrupt shoulder, q, which, when the barrel is turned upon the said pivot, strikes against the end of the rod and thrusts it rearward, as indicated by the arrows in Figs. 4 and 5. The pivot e is prevented from being withdrawn from its position in the recessed projection b of the barrel by a screw-pin, r, adapted to an annular groove cut in the said pivot; the extractor-rod k is similarly prevented by a pin, s, from being drawn outward in the direction of the arrow from the stem a. The extractor is forced outward, as above described, by the shoulder q of the eccentric pivot e, and it may be either pushed inward by hand, be permitted to fall inward by its own weight, or be acted on by a suitable spring. The usual notched projection t by which the cylinder is turned through the medium of a finger, which receives its motion from the hammer, is, in the present instance, secured to the rear face of the plate l of the extractor, instead of directly to the cylinder, as in ordinary revolvers, and a rounded projection, k', of the extractor, at the rear of the said notched projection, is adapted to a recess, u, of the frame when the barrel is closed, and thus serves to brace or support the hollow stem a and to reduce the strain of the cylinder upon the same when the fire-arm is discharged.

To load the fire-arm, the spring-catch i is pressed back with one hand to unlock the barrel, while with the other hand the barrel is turned sufficiently upon the eccentric pivot to entirely expose the rear end of the cylinder, the chambers in which are then filled with ordinary metallic cartridges x. The barrel is then closed and locked between the curved projection h of the frame and the spring-catch i, as before described, the rounded end k' of the extractor striking against the inclined edges of the recess u of the frame in the act of closing the barrel, and thus forcing the extractor-case up to and into the recess at rear of the cylinder.

When all of the cartridges have been charged the barrel is opened as before, but greater extent, in order that the shoulder q of eccentric pivot may strike the end of the extrac rod, and thus force the plate l outward from cylinder, as shown in Figs. 4 and 5, the said pl pushing before it, and partially withdrawing the chambers of the cylinder the whole num of empty cartridge-cases, which are thus pu forward to a sufficient extent to enable the be entirely withdrawn by hand prior to the loading of the fire-arm and the closing up of barrel.

I claim—

1. A revolving fire-arm in which the barr hung to the frame and arranged to turn ec trically upon a vertical axis, substantiall herein described.

2. The vertical eccentric pivot e, so arra in respect to the centers of the barrel and rev ing cylinder that the rear end of the said cyli can be brought close up to and turned out from the frame, without risk of striking the ter, and without involving the usual necessi rounding off its corners.

3. The combination, substantially as herei scribed, of the eccentric pivot e and its sho or shoulders with the cartridge-extractor D

In testimony whereof I have signed my to this specification in the presence of two scribing witnesses.

Witnesses: CHRISTIAN SHARF
WM. A. STEEL,
JOHN K. RUPERTUS.

UNITED STATES PATENT OFFICE.

CHRISTIAN SHARPS, OF PHILADELPHIA, PENNSYLVANIA.

IMPROVEMENT IN BREECH-LOADING FIRE-ARMS.

Specification forming part of Letters Patent No. **137,625**, dated April 8, 1873; application filed July 14, 1871.

To all whom it may concern:

Be it known that I, CHRISTIAN SHARPS, of Philadelphia, county of Philadelphia, State of Pennsylvania, have invented Improvements in Breech-Loading Fire-Arms, of which the following is a specification:

Nature and Object of my Invention.

My invention consists of certain improvements in breech-loading fire-arms, too fully explained hereafter to need preliminary description; the main object of my invention being the production of a safe breech-loading fire-arm, which can be rapidly loaded and discharged.

Description of the Accompanying Drawing.

Figure 1, Sheet 1, is a longitudinal sectional view of my improved breech-loading fire-arm; Fig. 2, the same, showing the breech opened; Fig. 3, a plan view of Fig. 1; Figs. and 5, Sheet 2, sections on the line 1 2, Fig. , showing the hammer and firing-pin and safety device for preventing the accidental movement of the firing-pin and premature discharge of the cartridge; Figs. 6 and 7, sections on the line 3 4, Fig. 3, showing the operation of the cartridge-extractor; and Fig. 8, a view representing a modification of the safety device connected with the firing-pin.

General Description.

A represents the frame of the fire-arm, and B the barrel, the former being recessed at the rear of the barrel for the reception of the breech-piece and parts connected therewith, and being secured to or forming part of a stock, C, within which is arranged an ordinary gun-lock, of which D is the hammer and E the trigger. The breech-piece F consists of a solid block of metal, fitted snugly within the recess of the frame, and hinged or pivoted within the latter to a pin, , which passes through the opposite sides of the frame, and permits the said breech to be raised and closed against the end of the barrel, as shown in Fig. 1, or to be thrown back from the same, as seen in Fig. 2. The breech-piece has a smooth, straight face, b, which fits accurately and closely against the rear of the barrel and flanged end of the cartridge; and the upper and rear portion of the said breech is

formed on a curve described from the center of the pin a, and is adapted to and arranged to turn in close proximity to the correspondingly-curved rear end c of the recess in the frame. A curved cam-like projection, q, Figs. 3 and 4, is formed on the side of the breech adjacent to the hammer for the purpose of acting upon and lifting the latter to the position of half-cock during the opening of the said breech, as will be more fully explained hereafter. A curved lever, G, bent to such a form as to serve as a trigger-guard, is hung to the pin d in the lower portion of the frame A beneath the breech-piece, and is acted on by a spring, e, secured to the frame, which tends to maintain it in the raised position shown in Fig. 1. This lever G is connected by a link, H, to a bolt, J, which is adapted to and has a limited sliding movement in a recess, f, formed for its reception in the rear portion of the breech-piece. The extent of this movement of the bolt is determined by slots g g, formed in the opposite sides of the breech-piece, and into which project the ends of the pin h, by which the said bolt is connected to the link.

When the breech is closed, as shown in Fig. 1, it is backed against the end of the barrel by means of the bolt J, which is then interposed between the said breech and an inclined shoulder, i, of the frame. In opening the breech by means of the lever G the bolt J is, during the first portion of the movement of the lever, drawn inward from the shoulder i, so as not to interfere with the movement of the said breech, as will be fully described hereafter.

The center-fire cartridge x, which is adapted, as usual, to the rear open end of the barrel, is exploded by means of a firing-pin, K, arranged to slide in an opening in the breech, and having, at its rear end, an inclined enlargement or head, k, which is struck and thrust forward by the descending hammer.

The premature discharge of the cartridge by means of the firing-pin is prevented by a dog, m, hung to the frame A, acted on by a suitable spring, and arranged to catch and hold back the said firing-pin until it is lifted, by means of the hammer, before the latter strikes the firing-pin. (See Figs. 4 and 5.)

The cartridge extractor or ejector consists of a

simple arm, L, adapted to a recess in the frame at one side and in front of the breech-piece, which is also slightly recessed for its reception, the said extractor being hung to the same pin *d* to which the operating-lever G is pivoted, and being operated in such a manner as to extract or eject the cartridge after the opening of the breech by means of a shoulder, *n*, on the said lever, which, during the last portion of the movement of the latter, strikes a projection, *n'*, of the extractor, and thus starts the same, the movement of the extractor being completed by means of a spring, *p*, with which it is provided. (See Figs. 6 and 7.)

In order that the operation of the fire-arm may be fully understood, let it be supposed that a cartridge has been introduced into the barrel, the breech closed and locked by means of the lever G and bolt J, and the hammer cocked. On the descent of the latter the inclined end of the safety catch or dog *m* will first be struck and raised; as shown in Fig. 5, so as to release the firing-pin, and the latter will then be struck and thrust forward by the hammer and the cartridge exploded. The recoil will be taken up by the solid metal of the breech, the bolt J, and frame A; these several parts, as best observed in Figs. 1 and 6, being in close contact with each other, and the whole being locked, and in a measure wedged together, by means of the bolt J, which prevents any possibility of the turning or opening of the breech, and, by taking up the whole force of the recoil, relieves the strain which would otherwise be brought to bear upon the pivoting and connecting pins of the breech, link, and operating-lever. After the discharge of the cartridge the lever G is lowered in the direction of the arrow, Fig. 1. During the first portion of this movement the bolt J will be drawn back clear of the shoulder *i* and into the recesses in the breech, so as to unlock the latter, and as soon as the pin *h* has passed entirely through the slots *g g* of the breech, and the bolt has been thus drawn back, the said breech will, on the continuance of the movement of the lever in the same direction, be opened or thrown back, as shown in Fig. 2. The hammer will also, during this movement of the lever and breech-piece, be raised by the cam-like projection *q*

of the latter to the position of half-cock, and will not, therefore, offer any obstruction to the opening or closing of the said breech. During the last portion of the movement of the lever in the same direction, its shoulder *n* will strike the projection *n'* of the extractor L and turn the latter slightly in the direction of the arrow, Fig. 7, so as to start the cartridge-case, which is sometimes apt to stick in the barrel. The movement of the extractor in the same direction is completed by means of its spring *p*, which, after the starting of the cartridge-case by the positive movement of the operating-lever, suddenly ejects the said case, after which another loaded cartridge is inserted in the barrel. The breech is then closed by means of the operating-lever and locked, as before, by the bolt J, the breech as it is raised coming in contact with the extractor and pushing the same before it to its original position, Fig. 6.

Instead of employing the dog *m* as a device for holding back the firing-pin, the said dog may be dispensed with and the firing-pin be provided at one side with a lip, *s*, Fig. 8, adapted to an eccentric slot, *t*, formed in the frame A, the said lip, and consequently the firing-pin, being drawn back by passing through the eccentric slot when the breech is lowered or opened, and remaining drawn back when the said breech is closed, as indicated by the dotted lines.

Claims.

1. The curved cam-like projection *q* of the breech-piece, arranged to act upon and lift the hammer to the position of half-cock when the said breech-piece is opened, all substantially as specified.

2. The firing-pin K, so combined with and controlled by a cam-slot, *t*, dog *m*, or equivalent device, that it shall be drawn back by the same into the breech in the act of opening or closing the latter.

In testimony whereof I have signed my name to this specification in the presence of two subscribing witnesses.

CHRISTIAN SHARPS.

Witnesses:
WM. A. STEEL,
JOHN K. RUPERTUS.

C. SHARPS.
Breech-Loading Fire-Arms.

No. 137,625.   Patented April 8, 1873.

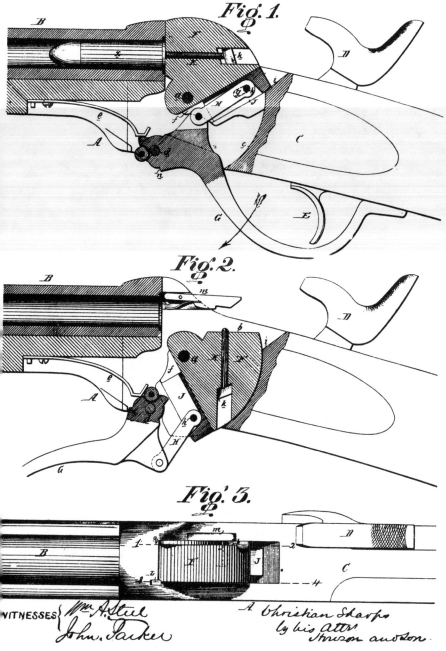

WITNESSES { Wm. A. Steel
             John. Parker

A Christian Sharps
by his attys
Johnson and Son.

AM. PHOTO-LITHOGRAPHIC CO. N.Y. (OSBORNE'S PROCESS)

2 Sheets--Sheet 2.

C. SHARPS.

Breech-Loading Fire-Arms.

No. 137,625. Patented April 8, 1873.

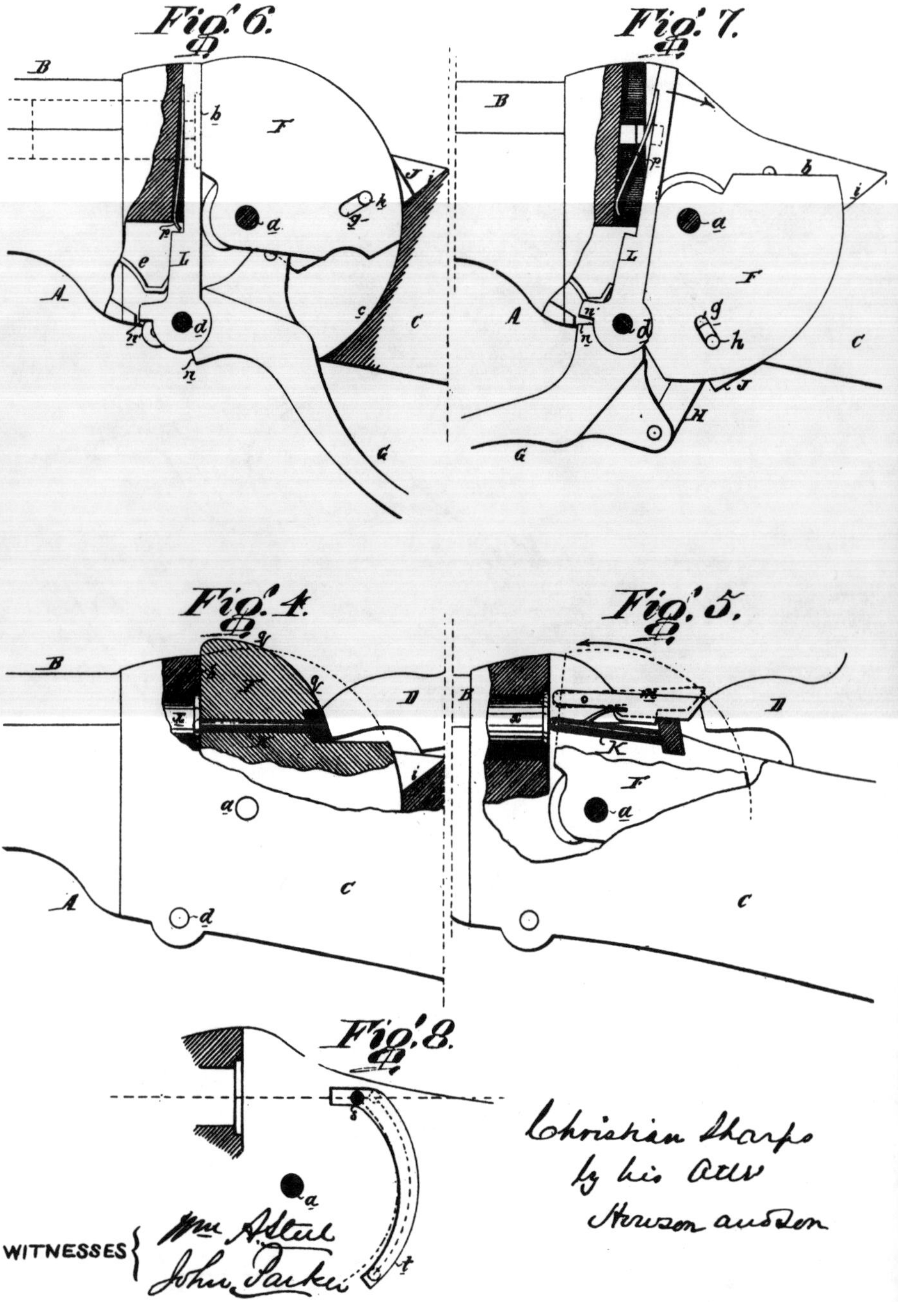
Fig. 6.
Fig. 7.
Fig. 4.
Fig. 5.
Fig. 8.

WITNESSES { Wm A Steel
John Parker

Christian Sharps
by his Atty
Arnison and Son

AM. PHOTO-LITHOGRAPHIC CO. N.Y. (OSBORNE'S PROCESS.)